Faith Walk

William P. Register, Sr.

WESTBOW
PRESS®
A DIVISION OF THOMAS NELSON
& ZONDERVAN

WestBow Press books may be ordered through booksellers or by contacting:

WestBow Press
A Division of Thomas Nelson & Zondervan
1663 Liberty Drive
Bloomington, IN 47403
www.westbowpress.com
1 (866) 928-1240

ISBN: 978-1-5127-7045-2 (sc)
ISBN: 978-1-5127-7047-6 (hc)
ISBN: 978-1-5127-7046-9 (e)

Library of Congress Control Number: 2016921634

Print information available on the last page.

WestBow Press rev. date: 3/7/2017

Contents

Introduction

A few years ago, I began writing a weekly, inspirational column for the leading newspaper in our county. That practice has continued and every week, the *Faith Walk* column appears in the paper.

Then, someone suggested that a compilation of these weekly articles would make a good book. From that suggestion, **Faith Walk**, this book, was created.

This book contains 145 of the weekly columns I have written. They were selected from the total collection as the ones that best represent the weekly messages I have contributed to the people in our county, via *Clay Today*, the newspaper that publishes them.

I wrote each article included in this book to encourage, challenge and teach the reader. My intention was to speak very basic truths to my original audience, who make up a socially and economically diverse community; therefore, I kept each article simple and basic.

One of the most requested articles in this book is titled, "Fellowship." It's found on page 53. Some of them are also very special to me. I particularly like the one that tells about the experiences of

1

H. G. Spafford and his family, from which came the song, *"It Is Well with My Soul."* My prayer is for each of them to deeply and personally minister to you.

I invite you to join me on this walk of faith. We are challenged daily to walk faithfully with our Savior. We need all the strength we can receive from the Holy Spirit to maintain our walk with Him. I hope this book will provide you with some of the strength you need to walk close to Him every day.

~William P. Register, Sr.

January – February – March

The First Step

I am planning to write a book. Actually, I have the concept for four books. I have the titles in mind and the overall idea for the content for each one. The fifth book—or it could be the first one— could be a collection of these Faith Walk columns that I have now written for more than two years. (This one is number 111 of my Faith Walk columns.)

My concept for each of these books is great, I believe. But I know that none of this glorious content that is so vivid in my mind will ever be written unless I start to work on them.

The first step toward getting to any goal is starting. If you do not take the first step on any journey you will never get to your destination or your goal.

I like the idea of thinking about these books. I just know that each of them will be great if I will only write them. That means starting, and that seems to be the hardest part of any worthwhile endeavor. No matter how long I think about writing a book, the job will never get done unless I start.

You cannot originate anything, you cannot improve anything, and you cannot do anything, until you start.

It seems that getting started is difficult because you know the path to completion is going to be hard work … and maybe pain and struggle.

An ancient wise man once said, "A journey of a thousand miles begins with a single step." So here I am. I know I will never finish a job that I do not start!

What do you believe the Lord is leading you to do? Are you failing to do it because you are fearful of the journey to complete the task? Is it hard? Time consuming? Does it mean you will have to give up some things you like to do so you will have time to do what you need to do?

It's challenging, but I know I—uh oh, I meant you—can do it. Let's get started doing what the Lord has called us to do.

New Things

A baby is born. A couple marry. A family moves to another state. A young man graduates from college. There are always new beginnings, and another segment of the future stretches before us.

It seems natural to think of things like these at this time in our calendar. We call the beginning of every year the "new year." Without having to do it only at the start of another year, God looks at our lives and is always ready to help us "start over again."

Someone said "He is the God of a second chance." And He is. He is also the God of third chances—fourth chances—fifth chances. In fact, His "love allowance" for us is unlimited.

He permits us to forget the past. I don't mean He just allows us to forget. I mean He enables us to forget the troubles and treacheries of the past and serve Him with a new start!

"Anyone who belongs to Christ has become a new person. The old life is gone; **a new life has begun!**" (2 Corinthians 5:17 NLT)

This is the Apostle Paul telling us that the Lord gives us a new start, or new beginning, when we come to Christ. This same servant of the Lord wrote, "Forgetting what is behind and straining toward what is ahead, I press on toward the goal to win the prize for which God has called me." (Philippians 3:13-14 NIV)

Forgetting the past. Pressing forward to the prize God has for us. That is the direction we are being given by the Spirit of the Lord every day.

"The future is as bright as the promises of God." - William Carey

When you accept a new start in your life and begin the pursuit of God's will, plan, and purpose for you, you are walking into a bright new light.

"Put on your new nature, created to be like God—truly righteous and holy." (Ephesians 4:24 NLT) This is not just a self-help resolution. This is a calling of the Spirit which He enables us to fulfill.

Walking By Faith

The title of this book is *Faith Walk*. What does it really mean to "walk by faith" every day? Paul wrote, "We walk by faith, not by sight." Again, he said, "The righteous shall live by faith."

In the Scriptures, the word "walk" means our daily living. "Faith" means believing what God's Word says is true regardless of what you have physically seen or personally experienced.

That seems simple enough. Live by trusting God regardless of the events and circumstances of your daily life.

Nothing is simple. That is a rule for understanding life!

Therefore, we face an onslaught of challenges to our faith in God. The challenges bring questions—uncertainties—doubt. Our faith always brings us back to this truth:

"And we know that for those who love God all things work together for good, for those who are called according to his purpose." (Romans 8:28 ESV)

When a calamitous situation strikes you—sickness, family crisis, unjust attacks, something that challenges your faith to its very core, and makes you want to question even the love of God, remember that you are living for the reward of an eternal life and not for rewards in this life.

I think one of the best things about going to Heaven is that we will be able to get all the answers to all our questions.

Just think, if you will just trust Him today, you will have the opportunity of having the wisdom of eternity revealed to you when you stand in His eternal presence.

> We'll talk it over in the bye and bye
> We'll talk it over, my Lord and I.
> I'll ask the reasons – He'll tell me why,
> When we talk it over in the bye and bye
>
>   – Ira Stanphil

Meanwhile, we live by faith and not by sight.

An Anniversary

That day was an anniversary of sorts. I had written 125 "Faith Walk" columns for Clay Today newspaper. It had been a great privilege to write a message every week for the citizens of Clay County, FL. I appreciate the partnership with Clay Today. I hope some of those columns offered encouragement and help.

In the 125 times I had written that column, I discussed many Bible themes and wrote about great Christian hymns with powerful personal messages. Mostly I think I endeavored to write encouraging messages about walking with our Lord in the faithful life.

I think one of the most effective columns written was about the need for Christian fellowship. Over the years, I have had more direct comments about it than any other column. The most popular was a great story of two men teaching about the value of fellowship with fellow believers.

Another column that really affected me was about H. G. Spafford who wrote the wonderful hymn, "It Is Well with My Soul." It tells the story of Mr. Spafford's family dying when their ship sank while crossing the Atlantic. Out of his great grief and loss, he wrote that wonderful hymn that has blessed and encouraged so many people.

I frequently meet people who tell me they read "Faith Walk." Some have even told me they read it weekly. Those are always encouraging words. After 125 articles, the well tends to run dry, but I continually asked the Lord to give me something that would minister to people as they read it.

I sincerely hope this book is a blessing to you. I pray it will continue to bless you—I wrote it to you from my heart.

Beginnings

This is a time when we think of beginnings, or making a new start.

I believe God grants second chances in many things. In fact, I would even say He often gives third, fourth, fifth, and many more opportunities to start over.

He gave Simon Peter forgiveness and a new start to serve Him.

He gave Saul of Tarsus a chance to start over.

You could say that the Lord gave these men and many others the chance to start their lives again. From the pits of failure to the pinnacle of victory, the Lord lifted them with new beginnings.

This must have been what Jesus meant when he answered the Pharisee, Nicodemus, who came to Him with life-shaking questions. Nicodemus (John chapter 3) came to Jesus at night to find the way to eternal life. He was shocked when Jesus said to him, "You must be born again." Jesus was saying that one could start life over again in a way that is as clear and definite as birth. This is the New Birth Jesus taught as the way to salvation and Heaven.

The New Birth is also the beginning of a new life. Therefore, it is a point for starting over in a life lived for the Lord.

Simon Peter followed his insulting denial of Jesus by repenting and starting over at the Lord's invitation. Saul of Tarsus encountered Jesus while he was on the way to persecute the followers of Jesus. He identified himself to Saul and gave him the chance to start his life over. It is to the credit of both of these men that they accepted the invitation of Jesus to leave their past and start a new life looking toward the future.

It was Saul, who became the Apostle Paul, who said, "Forgetting the past and looking forward to what lies ahead, I press on to reach the end of the race and receive the heavenly prize." (Philippians 3:13-14 NLT)

Many have started their lives over with a fresh opportunity from the Lord. You and I can, too.

Trust

Trust is relying on the character, ability, strength, or truth of someone or something. When you trust, you are completely leaning on someone else.

There is about 20 year's difference in my brother and me in age. Years ago when he was about five years old, I started playing a game with him. I put him on an elevated porch and told him to jump into my arms. He was about four or five feet above the ground and it must have looked like a long way down to him.

I encouraged him to run and jump and assured him that I would catch him. He ran right up to the edge but quickly stopped. He stood there looking down. I told him to back up, run to the edge and jump and I would catch him. He backed up and ran toward the edge of the porch. At the edge, he suddenly stopped again. It was too far down for him to take a chance! After several attempts, he gathered his courage, ran to the edge, and jumped! I caught him in the air, swung him around to his great delight, and put him down on the ground.

He ran quickly back up on the porch, ran toward the edge and shouted, "Catch me" and jumped. Once he knew he could trust me, he wanted to play repeatedly—and he could trust me. I caught him every time he jumped.

When you know you can trust the Lord, you want to keep trusting Him more and more. Once you know you can completely rely on Him, you have a foundation and an anchor. The more you trust Him, the more you want to trust Him!

> Jesus, Jesus, how I trust Him!
> How I've proved Him o'er and o'er;
> Jesus, Jesus, precious Jesus!
> Oh, for grace to trust Him more!
> "'Tis So Sweet to Trust in Jesus" - lyrics by Louisa M. R. Stead

I recently received an email message from an unknown friend. The email just said, "Trust in the Lord with all your heart and do not lean on your own understanding." (Proverbs 3:5 ESV).

Sweet confirmation of what I've known, but so nice to be reminded!

My Best Friend

My dearest friend died last week. He was a man that I was very close to in a wonderful friendship for sixty years. That is almost a complete lifetime.

I shared a lot with my friend. We were roommates all through college. He was the best man in my wedding. I shared his sorrow with him when his first wife died. After her death, we drove weekly the hundred miles that separated us to spend time together to alleviate his loneliness. He was faithfully with me (again closing the hundred mile gap) when I was seriously ill requiring an extended stay in the hospital.

Through the years, we talked regularly on the phone. We met every year in a personal reunion.

At his funeral, several of his family members said to me, "He loved you." And I replied, "I loved him too." Two men—lifelong friends—both from the "old school," but unashamed to say that we loved each other.

In a lifetime, most people have very few true friends. Many never have even one lifelong, true friend. I have been blessed to have some very good friends. I had to say goodbye to one of the very closest of them last week.

He was as close to me as a brother. I miss him. I will miss William Loftis Satterfield for the rest of my life.

There is a friend that we will never lose. He is the friend who is always with us—He never forsakes us. He has promised that He will always be with us. He is that friend who "sticks closer than a brother." (Proverbs 18:24 ESV)

Jesus is that friend. He is a husband to the widow. He is a father to the orphan. He is Savior to the sinner.

If you will allow Him, He will be your friend. He said, "I do not call you servants … I have called you friends …" (John 15:15 AMP)

The Love Walk

1 Corinthians 13 may be the greatest chapter in the Bible. While there could be dissent on this, I believe there would be agreement that this chapter is the greatest chapter on practical Christianity.

If you will live the love walk as described in this chapter, you will have success in the relationships of your life.

It starts with the declaration that great spiritual gifts are worthless without love. (Verses 1 & 2)

Then we learn that generosity and sacrifices have no value without love. (Verse 3)

Love gives up the right to be right. (Verses 4-7)

Even great spiritual gifts will end. However, love will endure forever. (Verses 8-10)

Faith, hope, and love endure forever. Great sermons have been preached on each of these gifts of God, and rightfully so. They are each powerful gifts from God for the fulfillment of our spiritual destiny. As wonderful, powerful, and glorious as each of them is, the greatest of all is LOVE.

Faith even works by love. (Galatians 5:6) Our foundation is more love than faith. If you have love, you will have faith.

The fruit of the Holy Spirit, God's personal presence in our lives, is love! (Galatians 5:22) From this precious spiritual fruit comes joy, peace, patience, kindness, goodness, and faithfulness.

I strongly recommend that you read 1 Corinthians 13. Get a Bible in an English Standard Version, New International Version, or New Living Translation and read this chapter. Then read it several more times. If you will live by it, your life and relationships will be powerful.

Love never fails. The greatest of all is love. This is the way to live every day. Start the New Year on the right path.

The Race

Run the race. Stay the course. Never give up.

These statements have been used many times to speak of persevering to the final victory. The writers of the New Testament often compare the Christian life to a race.

It is an unusual race we are running. There is a finish line at the end of this race. There is a great victory for the winners of this race. However, it is a race that is run in a different way from the normal race.

Usually the fastest runner wins a race. He is the one who crosses the finish line first. There is always a prize of some kind for the winner of the race. Sometimes others in the race may win a prize.

This race of life is different. The main difference is this. Everyone who finishes the race wins the prize. That prize is an incorruptible crown of life.

The writer of Hebrews speaks of our race this way: " …let us also lay aside every weight and sin which clings so closely and let us run with endurance the race that is set before us, looking to Jesus, the founder and perfecter of our faith …" (Hebrews 12:1-2 ESV)

Endurance is the requirement for victory in this race. Patience is another word that describes how we endure.

We want to win the race of life. The victory comes by enduring patience, which means we never give up. We persevere until we cross that final victory line.

This imagery or metaphor of our life for Christ being the running of a race should help to keep us strong every day. Whatever obstacles arise to block your way, remember you must finish strong. Paul wrote to the Corinthians to carefully continue and never stop until this course is finished. (1 Corinthians 9:24-27)

Jesus said, "The one who endures to the end will be saved." (Matthew 24:13 ESV) There it is again. Endure. Persevere. Continue. Never quit. And you will win in the race of life.

Dry Bones

Ezekiel was a prophet in the Old Testament to whom God gave messages for the Jewish people. One of the great things Ezekiel prophesied was the restoration of the nation of Israel, as recorded in Chapter 37 of the book of Ezekiel, in the Bible.

God showed Ezekiel a large valley filled with dry bones. Having him look out over the valley, the Lord asked him, "Can these bones live?" Ezekiel answered, "Lord, you know." What the prophet saw was impossibility. No, the dead, dry bones could not live again in the natural. Ezekiel knew it would take a supernatural act.

The meaning of God restoring the dry bones to life is that God promises and prophesies the restoration of Israel. In 1948, the nation of Israel was re-born. Students of the Bible view the restoration and the continuation of Israel as God's miracle. He has in fact, breathed life into the dry bones in the valley.

While the restoration of Israel is clearly the primary meaning of Ezekiel 37, it is also an allegory teaching that our Lord is a God of restoration for us. The same God of Israel who made the dry bones of Ezekiel's valley live again is the God who is ready to turn your dry bones into new life.

The despair, defeat, and deterioration of your life are reversible. God's merciful act of restoration is the miracle answer for you. Take all the unwanted burdens of your life and cast them into the valley. They are just "dry bones" in the plan of God for your life. Put your total trust in God! He can, and will, turn your dry bones into a living victory of restoration.

Give your dry bones to Him. Let God breathe the breath of life into you. You will find that His restoration is the power of victory for you.

Are You Ready?

Recently I read an article about people who have won large amounts of money in a lottery. Most states have lotteries now and there are even national lotteries with prizes of hundreds of millions of dollars.

Some of the stories of the winners are heartbreaking. One man said, "Winning the lottery was the worst thing that has ever happened to me."

It has been said that for every person who fails God because of inability to handle adversity, there are many more who fail Him because they cannot deal with prosperity.

We need to prepare for whatever life brings us whether judged as good or bad. It takes great grace to deal with either a surge of prosperity or an attack of fiery trials.

I know you are thinking, "I would certainly rather deal with the trial of prosperity than to be tried by adversity."

The natural mind would think that. However, it is very sad when God allows us to receive wonderful benefits and we then allow the very blessings He has given us to draw us away from Him.

The young man who came to Jesus illustrates this well. He asked Jesus how to have eternal life. Jesus said, "Go and sell all that you have and give it to the poor. You will have treasure in heaven." The young man went away with great sorrow because he was very rich.

If the young man had agreed to do as Jesus said, I do not think it would have been required of him. The important thing that had to be determined was where his greatest values were.

Be ready to face any circumstance of life. God can give you grace to handle every issue in your life, if you walk closely with Him. The world may look at your life circumstances with pity or envy. That is not what is important. What is important is that you deal with every life issue as a child of God who trusts your heavenly Father to work His will and pleasure in your life.

Do Not Judge

Jesus was speaking to all of us when He said, "Do not judge and you will not be judged." This is one particular teaching that will bring you great peace if you will accept it. Incorrectly judging others adds a burden of responsibility that you do not have to carry.

Understand that the judgment He speaks about has nothing to do with legal issues. This is not instruction for the legal or judicial system. It is not personal direction for you in such issues as jury duty or testifying in a legal matter.

This instruction relates to others with whom your life intersects. It refers to all personal relationships whether in your family, workplace, church, or just in the interactions of your life with other individuals.

When you judge the motives of others, you put yourself in the position of God. This is really the danger area. Jesus referred to this when He spoke of having a log in your own eye while you point out the speck that is in your friend's eye! Few, if any, are qualified to pass personal judgment on anyone else. Definitely none of us is qualified to judge the motives of another.

The classic Scriptural illustration of this point is in John chapter 8. A woman was discovered involved in adultery. Religious leaders wanted to stone her, which was the punishment of the era. They came to Jesus with the woman and asked Him what should happen to her.

Jesus' answer was classic. He looked over the men standing there who had already formed their judgment of her. He said, "Let any one of you who is without sin be the first to throw a stone at her." (John 8:7 NIV) Then starting with the oldest one there to the youngest one, they left without doing anything.

Each one of them recognized his own lack of qualification to judge the sin of the woman. Those who had come to judge her were condemned by their own guilt.

Let's not carry this illustration too far. We all continuously need to look carefully at ourselves before we judge anyone else. If we were to do this, we would make more effort to correct our own faults before acting in judgment toward anyone else.

Contentment

"I have learned in whatever situation I am to be content."

The Apostle Paul wrote these words to the Philippian church. He wrote the epistle to that church from prison and he wanted to assure the Christians at Philippi that he was not in need. In fact, he was satisfied with his condition.

Compare the attitude of Paul with the expectations of many people today. Most people have a list of things they say it will take for them to be content. These are usually "things" they believe they need to have to be happy or content.

Paul had learned that things do not bring contentment, joy, and happiness. He knew that true contentment rests in trusting the Lord.

There is an area of contentment in life where we can live through our faith in Him. To do this, there are some things we need to understand. Here are some things for you to consider:

First, we cannot live in fear. Growing in the love of God is the antidote to fear. Many live in fear of the future unable to trust God for His will and plan. If we will develop God's love in our lives, fear will vanish. The Bible says, "There is no fear in love. But perfect love drives out fear ..." (1 John 4:18 NIV) We do not have to fear either life or death.

Second, we cannot live in the past. Most people have things they want to remember and things they want to forget. Any experiences that hold us to the past must be given up at the Cross.

Third, we must lean wholly on God's grace, which He expresses in us by His love and mercy.

These are beginning steps to living in joy, favor, and contentment.

"But godliness with contentment is great gain." (1 Timothy 6:6 NIV)

Champions

This week a college football team won the national championship in that sport. Very shortly, a professional football team will win a game that will designate them as champions of their sport. It happens in almost every level of every sport. It seems we have to have winners and losers.

The Scriptures promise that every Christian believer can be a champion. There are winners and losers in life and the Bible clearly says that through Jesus we can each be a winner. You need to understand the Scriptural definition of a winner—or champion.

Clearly, we are told that life is a battle and the believer will be under attack. Peter says we will face "fiery trials." (1 Peter 4:12) Paul told the Corinthians of many trials he had endured. That same Apostle warned the Ephesian church they must clothe themselves in the whole armor of God to be able to stand the attacks they would face. (Ephesians 6) However, he put it all in the context of victory when he said that regardless of the kind of trial or the strength of the attack, the believers are "more than conquerors" in Christ. (Romans 8:34-39)

We are not champions because we are stronger than others are. In fact, the Scripture tells us that our victory is in our weakness! It is in our own weakness that we become strong in Christ because we depend on Him. The more we depend on him, the stronger we are.

That is what leads us to true victory and championship. Jesus said it clearly: "Apart from me you can do nothing." (John 15:5 NIV)

"For the sake of Christ, then, I am content with weaknesses, insults, hardships, persecutions, and calamities. For when I am weak, then I am strong." (2 Corinthians 12:10 ESV)

You can be one of God's champions by totally leaning on Him and trusting Him for your strength.

Clean Out the Dirt

I have a pair of shoes that I just cannot bring myself to discard, although I have worn them for years. They have been re-soled more than one time. I have put on new heels several times. I keep them because they are comfortable and I like the style. They are old but still look stylish when they are polished and repaired.

When I recently stumbled through a small pile of dirt, I got sand in the lattice style leather of the shoes. Yes, both shoes. Because of the way the leather is styled on the shoes, the dirt is trapped under some of the strips of leather.

To polish these shoes properly, I know the first thing I must do is clean out the dirt. It will not be easy to get into all the little crevices created by the leather design but I know the shoes will never look just right until I do that.

If we want to be effective for God in our lives, one of the first things we have to do is clean out the dirt! The dirt is sin. For us to be able to live the joyful life of spiritual success that we want to live, sin must be removed.

I keep looking at my shoes and I know I need help with this job. Therefore, I will take them to an expert to get the job done right.

We cannot just clean up our own lives. We need expert help to get that done. Jesus is the One who can help us. He provides us righteousness not just reformation. In Him we can have a transformed life. (2 Corinthians 5:17)

William P. Register, Sr.

Scripture is full of information on holy living. I will give you just two statements from the Bible. Jesus said, "The truth will set you free." (John 8:32 NIV) He continues and says, "If the Son sets you free, you will be free indeed." (John 8:36 NIV)

Meet Jesus at the eternal altar—the Cross. That is where He will clean out all the dirt from your life.

Amazing Grace

The dictionary gives us this definition of grace: "unmerited divine assistance given man for his regeneration or sanctification." Therefore, grace is God's favor. It is "unmerited and undeserved favor."

The most extraordinary expression of God's grace is Salvation.

Salvation is divine. It is the result of His grace. "For by grace you have been saved through faith. And this is not your own doing; it is the gift of God." (Ephesians 2:8 ESV)

God's grace is the source of our salvation. Salvation is a gift; it cannot be earned.

"…not a result of works, so that no one may boast." (Ephesians 2:9 ESV)

Grace, grace, God's grace,
Grace that will pardon and cleanse within;
Grace, grace, God's grace,
Grace that is greater than all our sin!
"Grace Greater Than All Our Sin" by Julia H. Johnston

It is grace—God's favor—that gives us strength to live an overcoming life daily. That is the victory of the Lord in us. When Paul sought the Lord three times to deliver him from his "thorn in the flesh," the word came back to him from God saying, "My grace is sufficient for you."

Then the Lord said to Paul "my power is made perfect in weakness." When we are weak in our own strength, God's grace is our power. It is when we are weakest that we are strongest by God's grace.

Probably the most famous hymn ever written is "Amazing Grace." The author, John Newton, spent much of his early life as a slave trader. By God's grace, he was saved and left that despicable trade.

Many questioned the use of the word "wretch" in the hymn's first verse. Newton knew it was appropriate!

> Amazing grace, how sweet the sound,
> That saved a wretch like me.
> I once was lost, but now am found,
> Was blind but now I see.

Good for Evil

Some things that Jesus taught us to do are very difficult. One of the basic teachings of Jesus is that we are to do good toward those who demonstrate animosity toward us. We are to return good for evil.

Jesus spoke of those who despitefully use us. He clearly told us that we are not to return the same thing to them that they spew upon us.

We think our response to malice demonstrated toward us should be to attack in return. Defend ourselves. Answer anything leveled against us. However, Jesus said we are to do the very opposite of that. His teaching was this:

> "You have heard that it has been said, 'You shall love your neighbor and hate your enemy.' But I say to you, Love your enemies, bless them that curse you, do good to them that hate you and pray for them who spitefully use you and persecute you ..." (Matthew 5:43-48 NKJV)

As we like to say, "That's easier said than done." And it is.

But following this direction by Jesus is not impossible. In fact, it is uplifting and strengthening for us when we act as Jesus taught us.

First, it gives us a chance to show God's love to others especially those who really need it.

Second, it allows us to know that we can have the strength of God's grace in our lives. (We can't live as Jesus taught us apart from the grace of God.)

We should practice the teachings of Jesus until integrated into our own personality. His words then become our first thought when negative situations occur by the actions of others.

This is the answer to insults, personal attacks, road rage, family discord, disloyalty, and betrayal when anyone acts or speaks against you.

Return good for evil.

God's Champions

Everyone wants to be a winner! We choose to view life as winning and losing. Too many of us look at all situations, seeing everyone as being either a winner or a loser.

God's word presents it differently. According to its teaching, the only losers are those who do not put their faith in Jesus Christ and live for Him.

The Scripture presents two ways for us to live. We choose to be wise or unwise—follow a narrow way or a broad way; live "in the flesh" or "in the Spirit." The choice we make for the path of our lives determines our triumphs or defeats.

New Testament teaching tells us we are overcomers in Christ. This is not a declaration of our own strength. It declares that we overcome through Christ. Paul said, "I can do all things through Christ who strengthens me." (Philippians 4:13 NKJV)

As God's word frequently tells us, there is abundance (overflowing) victory for us if we walk with Him. We are overcomers. We are victors. We are triumphant. To put it in today's vernacular, we are winners!

I said we are "more than" in the abundance of His grace and power.

Victorious Christians are God's champions! You can be one.

You do not have to live in defeat. Habits, addictions, oppressions, and mental and emotional attacks are defeated in Christ. You are not defeated. The attacks against you are defeated. You are the winner according to God's word for you!

Through inspiration of the Spirit Paul said, "In all these things we are more than conquerors through him that loved us." (Romans 8:37 NKJV)

Be a champion "through the One who loves us."

Appearance

You may think you cannot determine your own appearance, but you can. And you can do it without cosmetics or plastic surgery.

Proverbs 15:13 teaches that the face is an outer expression of your inner self. The way you can be sure that your inner quality makes you the person you want the world to see is to follow the Scripture. This is what Proverbs says: "A merry heart makes a cheerful countenance." (Proverbs 15:13 AKJV) The condition of your heart determines your countenance that the world sees.

"I don't like the looks of that man," Abraham Lincoln supposedly said to an aide. "A person can't help what he looks like, Mr. President," the aide replied. "Oh, yes, he can," Mr. Lincoln answered.

Lincoln was right. If your inner self is full of turmoil, distress and grief, it will show in your countenance. Inner peace, joy and a positive view of life based on the love and grace of God will also be reflected in the person you show to the people around you.

I like positive people. I'm sure you do, too. Who would not rather be around someone who expresses joyful, happy thoughts? In fact, I look for those people so that I can spend time with them.

You probably do the same thing even though you may not realize you are doing it. It is just more pleasant to be around a joyful, happy person.

Now, the next thing is for you to be that person with whom others want to fellowship. Keep in mind that you can determine the quality of your inner self. And that is what will determine what others see in you.

Proverbs 4:23 says "Keep your heart with all diligence; for out of it are the issues of life." (AKJV) That is the standard. When you do this you will look better, gain friends and enjoy your life.

"The *outcome* of your life will be determined by your *outlook* on life." (unknown)

Ponder Your Motives

Proverbs 12:15 warns that the way of a fool is right in his own eyes. A foolish person is one who thinks he is right in everything he does, refusing to listen to advice and not tolerating the opinion of others. The rule of his life is to be inflexible, demanding his own way.

Henry Ford made the Model T, an excellent car that dominated the market for many years. He was original and innovative when he founded his automobile manufacturing company, based largely on the concept of an assembly line. His assembly line had no room for anything but a black Model T Ford car. He was totally product-oriented. Ford wanted to fill the world with his Model T cars. However, when people started coming to him saying, "Mr. Ford, we'd like a different color car," he purportedly answered, "You can have any color you want as long as it's black!" That's when the decline started. That's when his company opened a wide door for competitors.

Being single minded can be good. Jesus commended such an attitude when supporting the right issue or cause. We must be very careful, however, that we do not identify our stubbornness as determination. We cannot allow the mistake of confusing inflexibility with strength.

When Jesus speaks of our eye being "single" (Matthew 6:22-23 KJV), He is referring to what we would call being "single minded."

If our purposeful pursuit is for righteousness, we are abundantly blessed. It is also possible to be unrighteous in a single-minded fashion. To stand inflexibly for total righteousness is noble. However, most of the positions we take for our causes are not for righteousness sake, but moreover to try to prove we are right.

It is important to know the difference between being stubborn and being right. Read the first paragraph again (Proverbs 12:15), and ponder your own motives.

God's Plan for You, His Child

There is a wonderful record in the Bible that perfectly illustrates God's plan for the life of every one of His children.

It is the story of Joseph. Due to envy and jealousy, Joseph's brothers had sold him into slavery. Imagine! His own brothers sold him as a slave!

Through a period of years, Joseph maintained his faith in God. Eventually God vindicated him and guided his advancement to the position of prime minister of Egypt. And then, as God so often does, He allowed events to bring Joseph and his brothers together again.

The brothers were pleading for help because their homeland was in a great famine and Egypt was overflowing with abundance due to the wisdom of Joseph. When his brothers recognized that he was the brother they had grossly betrayed so many years before, they were afraid that Joseph in his position of authority and political power would punish them in retribution for their evil deed against him.

Because God had promoted him, Joseph was in a position to exact any penalty he wanted against his brothers. What did he do? He forgave them, honored them and blessed them.

He showed the same forgiveness to them that God had shown to him. Joseph had risen from slave to become the chief executive of the greatest kingdom of his day because of the favor of God.

Joseph had the grace to forgive his brothers because He had trusted God through his life of trials. He was able to do this because he had the correct viewpoint of God's plan for him. He expressed that view to his brothers when he told them, "You intended to harm me, but God intended it all for good." (Genesis 50:20 NLT)

God has a good plan for you. If you keep your faith in Him through all the issues that come, God will fulfill that plan and bring you to the wonderful place in life that He has for you.

"For I know the plans I have for you," declares the LORD, "plans to prosper you and not to harm you, plans to give you hope and a future." (Jeremiah 29:11 NIV)

God's Requirements

Many things are complicated and difficult to understand. Often, however, even the most important things are very simple. Here is a statement from the Bible that expresses eternally important truth in a very simple way.

"He has shown you, O man, what is good; And what does the LORD require of you but to do justly, To love mercy, And to walk humbly with your God?" (Micah 6:8 NKJV)

These are simple but profound words. To know what God expects of us in this is to gain understanding and wisdom, and here it is:

Act justly—Integrity and honesty are still admirable qualities in any person's life. God expects us to live (i.e., act) with fairness and justice in everything we do.

It is not enough for us to hold high beliefs; God expects us to act on noble beliefs and by doing so we demonstrate the sterling character that develops from knowing and doing the right things.

Love mercy—"Compassionate treatment of those in need or distress" is the definition of "mercy" that I appreciate. What greater quality could an individual have than to love mercy?

Caring for others who may be deprived and downtrodden is a great expression of Christian character. I always think of the story of the Good Samaritan when I think of mercy. You know the Bible account of the good neighbor who acted in love and mercy when he helped the person in great need.

Mercy means forgiving. How can you hold grudges against others and be merciful at the same time? You cannot. It is impossible.

Walk humbly with God—This is the measure of a true follower of Jesus Christ. Nothing greater can be said of anyone than "he walked humbly with God."

God Knows Best for Us

Have you ever asked God for something and then realized you did not want your prayer answered?

You may have prayed, "Lord, grant this at any cost" or "Lord, do whatever it takes." Then you realized the enormous consequences a prayer like that could bring if it were answered.

It is a good thing God does not always take us at our word. He tempers the things we say with His mercy and understanding. And He always gives us grace.

He will also let us change our minds. I thank Him for that!

He knows us better than we know ourselves and we should thank Him every day that He does.

Sometime in your past, you may have told God you wanted Him to end it all for you. You prayed for him to take you from this world, but He didn't do it. Now you are glad He did not grant your request.

Jesus said, "Your Father knows what you need before you ask Him." (Matthew 6:8 NIV)

How wonderful it is to have such a Heavenly Father. He knows us; He loves us; He wants to bless us with full, joyful lives. And if we will walk with Him as His obedient children, He will withhold no good thing from us.

"The LORD bestows favor and honor. No good thing does he withhold from those who walk uprightly." (Psalm 84:11 ESV)

Walk with Him today. Talk with Him. Listen to Him. He knows you and He loves you. Do not doubt it. You will have a wonderful day every day that you put your life in His hands.

Someone Cares About You

Have you ever faced a time of deep personal sorrow? Someone very close to you died unexpectedly. You were diagnosed with an untreatable illness. Betrayal terminated a very personal relationship.

How did you deal with it? Some people turn to drugs, alcohol, or some other crutch that makes their problem worse.

Looking for answers in the wrong places produces the wrong answers.

Most often, the answer we need comes through a person. In the search for the answer to a deep sorrow, sometimes we put trust in the wrong person and, when he or she cannot be what we need, the problem is made worse.

When we are in the deepest sorrows of our life, we can always find the answers in Someone. When it seems there is no answer and there cannot be an answer, there is always One who can fill the chasm of sorrow or grief that has overwhelmed us.

He is a Light in darkness; a bright and shining Star in the dark midnight sky; the Rose blooming in the thicket of thorns. He is the Friend who will be closer to you than anyone else possibly can be.

Does Jesus care when my heart is pained
Too deeply for mirth or song,
As the burdens press,
And the cares distress,

And the way grows weary and long?
O yes, He cares, I know He cares,
His heart is touched with my grief;
When the days are weary,
The long night dreary,
I know my Savior cares.
- "Does Jesus Care?" by Frank E. Graeff

Turn to the One who loves you more than anyone else can love you. He is your Comforter and He is waiting to hear from you.

Fellowship

On a cold winter evening, two Christian men were sitting before a cozy fireplace, warming themselves. They were discussing their Christian lives and experiences.

The younger man expressed the reasons he did not believe attending church services was important to his Christian experience. The older, more experienced man listened carefully to the younger man's excuses. By this time, the flames of the fire had diminished and the fireplace held only the glowing coals.

Carefully the older man reached out with the fireplace poker and pulled one coal away from the rest of the glowing coals. The one coal, separated from the others, was alone on the hearth. The fire in the single coal quickly died and instead of a bright red glow, the coal became cold and grey.

Nothing needed to be said. The younger man got the message.

When we separate ourselves from the fellowship of Christian believers, we give up one of the great benefits of the Christian life. The fellowship of other believers is one of the invisible strengths that God has given His people. In corporate worship, we draw strength from the Lord by the encouragement of one another.

One of the most powerful statements the Apostle John made is in his first epistle. He says if we walk in the light of Jesus' presence and teaching " …we have fellowship with each other and the blood of Jesus, His Son, cleanses us from all sin." (1 John 1:7 NLT)

The fellowship of Christian believers is a gift of the father to His children. We deprive ourselves of God's best when we do not meet faithfully with others who share our Love for the Lord.

This is why Scripture teaches us to continue assembling ourselves together and exhorting one another with encouragement. (Hebrews 10:25) It is signally important that you meet with fellow Christians to worship together and encourage each other.

Finding Your Way

An old story about the city slicker and the farmer brings a smile. It seems the city slicker was driving on back roads and had become confused about his location when he saw an old farmer hoeing in the field. He stopped, got out of his car, and went toward the farmer to ask for his help.

"Can you tell me how far it is to the next town?" he asked. The old farmer paused, looked around a little, and replied, "I don't reckon I know." So the city slicker asked, "How far is it to the main highway?" Again, the farmer answered, "I don't reckon I know." Exasperated, he said to the farmer, "You don't know much, do you?" The farmer quickly said, "I know I ain't lost."

Do you know where you are today? Have you become confused on your journey while trying to find the way to your long desired destination?

Stop today and ask directions.

God has a roadmap for you and He will share it with you if you ask Him. That map is His plan for you and he wants you to know it.

"Your own ears will hear him. Right behind you a voice will say, 'This is the way you should go,' whether to the right or to the left." (Isaiah 30:21 NLT)

The Scriptures tell us many times that God will show us His path and guide us on it. A classic word from the Lord is Proverbs

3:6. "In all your ways acknowledge him, and he shall direct your paths." (NKJV)

If today your life is not what you want it to be, turn yourself over to the Lord and let Him direct you. He will show you the road you are to travel in order to reach the right destination.

How to Reach Your Destination

A man, who was travelling in an unfamiliar area, realized that he was lost. He stopped to ask directions from a man who looked like he might be familiar with the territory.

He told the man his destination and asked if he could give him directions to get there. Trying to help the traveler, the man said, "Well, if you go to the next crossroads and turn right … no, no, you need to drive straight down the road until you get to the gas station. Oh wait, that's not it. Here's what you do, turn around and go back the way you came until you see a big oak grove, then you turn … oh wait, that won't do it … hmmm, let me think a minute."

He pondered, scratched his head, looked perplexed, and then said, "Stranger, I don't think you can get where you're going from here."

How do you get to a desired destination when you don't know where you are? That depends more on your destination than your present location.

When Jesus was preparing His disciples for His death and physical departure from this world, He said to them, "I am going there to prepare a place for you. You know the way to the place where I am going."

A disciple answered Him, "Lord, we don't know where you are going, so how can we know the way?"

Jesus gave His classic answer, "I am the way, the truth and the life. No one comes to the Father except through me." (John 14:6 NKJV)

The way to the Father, to Heaven, to eternal life, is a person. You can meet that person wherever you are right now! He is the way to where you want to go.

It is not that Jesus knows the way or can tell you the way. Jesus *is* the way!

Ready For Heaven?

The Pastor was preaching about Heaven. He became very excited about the prospect of going to Heaven and he tried to communicate his sincere excitement of future hope to the congregation. Deeply involved in stressing to his congregation the joy of going to Heaven, he decided on interaction.

He shouted to the people, "Everyone who wants to go to Heaven, raise your hand!" Everyone in the church raised his hand except one man.

Surprised, the Pastor said again, "If you want to go to Heaven, raise your hand now!" All except the same man quickly raised a hand.

Now he was exasperated. He could not understand why this one man would not want to go to Heaven. He determined to be more decisive. He shouted, "Everyone who wants to go to Heaven, stand up now!"

All stood except the one man who had not raised his hand. Thoroughly frustrated and confused, the preacher pointed to the seated man. "Brother," he said, "don't you want to go to Heaven when you die?"

Instantly the man stood. "Pastor," he said, "I'm sorry I misunderstood you. Yes, I want to go to Heaven when I die, but I thought you were getting up a load to go *now*!"

There is a difference in being prepared for Heaven and being ready to go. Because you are prepared does not mean that you are ready to go this moment. Being prepared does not require you to want to leave this earth now.

I recommend that you be prepared for the promise Jesus made to you if you trust Him. Jesus said, " ...I go to prepare a place for you. And if I go and prepare a place for you, I will come again and take you to myself ..." (John 14:2-4 ESV)

If you are prepared by your faith in Jesus as your Savior, you will be ready when the Lord calls you into your Heavenly home.

I believe in Heaven. I am prepared now to go there. When He calls me, I will be ready to meet Him.

A Chosen Vessel

One of our greatest poets and hymn writers was Fanny Crosby. She wrote more than 8,000 hymns in her lifetime.

Frances Jane "Fanny" Crosby was born in 1820. She died in 1915 at the age of 95. That was a very long life in her day.

Some of the great hymns that she wrote are "Blessed Assurance," "Sweet Hour of Prayer," "Pass Me Not O Gentle Savior," "I Am Thine O Lord," "Near the Cross," and "I Shall Know Him." Her ministry of hymnology has blessed many thousands of people for many years. People sing all of these songs still today.

Fanny Crosby lost her eyesight at six weeks of age. She was blind her entire life!

Once a preacher sympathetically remarked, "I think it is a great pity that the Master did not give you sight when He showered so many other gifts upon you." She replied quickly, "Do you know that if at birth I had been able to make one petition, it would have been that I should be born blind?" "Why" asked the surprised minister. "Because when I get to heaven, the first face that shall ever gladden my sight will be that of my Savior!"

She was saying that her greatest desire and expectation was to see the face of her Savior in Heaven. She said, "His face will be the first one I will ever see!"

You may not have perfect conditions in your life. You may be dealing with distressing conditions that you have to overcome to perform daily duties. However, are you allowing impediments that burden you to keep you from effectively serving God?

Fanny Crosby rose above her blindness. She became an instrument in God's hands to bring great blessings to God's church and to the world.

Your hardships may slow you, but they cannot stop you unless you let them.

Totality

I was driving down a street one day when I came up behind an older van. It looked rather decrepit. Its age was apparent.

A large collection of bumper stickers obscured everything else on the back of the van. Every one of the bumper stickers had a Christian slogan.

All the ones you have seen were there. "Christians are not perfect just forgiven." "God is my Co-Pilot." "God is the Pilot; I'm the co-pilot." "In case of the Rapture this car will be driverless." "Honk if you love Jesus." There were so many bumper stickers that I thought the van was being held together by them.

Peeping out through the sticker collection, I could see two taillights and most of a license plate. Then I saw one bumper sticker that conspicuously stood out to me. In the lower right corner of the back of the van surrounded by all the Christian slogan messages there was a bumper sticker that said, "Bowlers have more fun."

Bowlers may have a lot more fun than non-bowlers may. I don't know, but I was impressed with someone who had 99% of the stickers on his van with a Christian message and had to have just one that spoke a secular message.

I got a good laugh. But I also got a message. It is important for us to realize that our consecration to the Lord must be total and absolute. It was a small, almost insignificant, point to observe the back of that van and see one secular sticker among a sea of Christian messages.

When you are totally sold out to the cause of Christ, there is no room for one little secret. You may think all the other good things you say and do hide it. But all those things (the many "Christian" bumper stickers) will not cover for the one thing you keep from God and hold onto for yourself.

This is not a message about bumper stickers whatever the message on them. It is not a message about a funny looking old van. It is a message about totally yielding to the Lord Jesus Christ.

Forgiveness

Forgiving us is the greatest thing God has ever done for us. He forgave all our sins when we believed in Jesus Christ as our Savior.

Possibly the most important thing He has instructed us to do in living for Him is to forgive others. In the "Lord's Prayer," where Jesus taught us how to pray, He included "Forgive us our trespasses as we forgive those who trespass against us."

He is not just teaching us to forgive those who have already sinned against us; He was teaching us to practice forgiveness as people continue to "trespass against us." We must do so for God to hear our prayers!

Jesus in fact said failure to forgive is a reason God will not hear our prayer. (Matthew 6:15; Mark 11:25)

Offenses have been committed against you that are hard for you to forgive. They may have happened long ago or they may have happened today. The time when any harm against you occurred does not matter. There is only one way to deal with it. That is to *forgive*! Time will never heal the harm. Only forgiveness is the healing balm.

The intensity of the offense does not matter! Whether it was egregious or slight, the response from you must be the same—total forgiveness.

Failure to forgive will disrupt your relationship with God. Failure to forgive will disrupt your personal peace of mind and spirit. Failure to forgive will affect your emotions and your personal relationships.

Knowing all this, Jesus taught us to practice forgiveness.

You do not wait for the offender to ask you for forgiveness. You recognize the purpose of God in teaching us to forgive is to bless and benefit us. Yes, on the human level, the person who will benefit the most in this great life walk of forgiving is the one who forgives, not the one who is forgiven.

Remember this because someone will offend you. Now you know what to do when that happens.

True Equality

"We hold these truths to be self-evident, that all men are created equal, that they are endowed by their Creator with certain unalienable Rights …," This statement is in one of the most treasured documents of the United States—the Declaration of Independence. That document is a powerful foundation stone for the political structure of our country.

But is it true that "all men are created equal?" Even politically, do all men (people) have the same God-given (unalienable) rights?

Certainly, people aren't created the same economically, physically, intellectually, or geographically.

So is there anything valid about this notion of equality? I answer "Yes." In the eyes of God, there is equal status for all of His creation.

First, God loves everyone equally. The Scripture says, "God so loved the world that He gave His only begotten Son that whoever believes …" (John 3:16 NKJV) So He declares His love for every person—the world. And He says that the result of that love is for everyone—whoever.

Next, Jesus died for the sins of every person. "He died for all." (2 Corinthians 5:15 ISV) "While we were still sinners, Christ died for us." (Romans 5:8 ESV)

An invitation to receive Christ was given at the close of a Gospel service in a church in the nation's capital. A high ranking, well-known government official responded and stood at the altar for prayer. An obviously poor man in disheveled apparel also walked forward for salvation and stood beside him. Some people in the church were alarmed that the poor man was standing beside the high-ranking man. Realizing the concern, the Pastor spoke about it to the congregation. He declared, "The ground is level at the foot of the cross."

And there is the answer. Everyone is equal in the cross of Jesus Christ.

Salvation Complete

From the Cross Jesus spoke powerful words. One of the most powerful things He said was, "It is finished." What did He mean by "it?"

It means the "once for all" offering to God, for all the sins of man, has been made. One has died as the sacrifice for the sins of all men for all time. " ...by his own blood ... He obtained eternal redemption for us." (Hebrews 9:12 NIV)

Securing our salvation in the plan of God requires nothing else. Since the price for sin was paid, we now can experience true salvation for eternity. God needs to do nothing else for our salvation. His plan is finished and it is in effect now.

Nothing needs added to the sacrifice of Jesus on the cross. His plan is finished. It is done in totality.

> "Jesus paid it all,
> All to Him I owe;
> Sin had left a crimson stain,
> He washed it white as snow."
>
> "Jesus Paid it All" by Elvina M. Hall

Every person's eternal salvation is only in Christ. We accept His sacrifice for us by God's grace and by our faith and the result is salvation. "For by grace you have been saved, through faith." (Ephesians 2:8 NIV)

"If you confess with your mouth that Jesus is Lord and believe in your heart that God raised him from the dead, you will be saved." (Romans 10:9 NKJV)

God's plan for salvation is this: Jesus died for everyone; therefore, everyone can be saved by faith in Him.

"...we have been sanctified (set apart and made holy) through the offering of the body of Jesus Christ once for all." (Hebrews 10:10 ASV)

"Just as I am, without one plea,
But that thy blood was shed for me,
And that thou bidst me come to thee,
O Lamb of God, I come, I come."

– "Just As I Am" by Charlotte Elliott

Doing Good

Mark Twain once said, "If you pick up a starving dog and make him prosperous, he will not bite you; that is the principal difference between a dog and a man."

This is a sharp indictment of man's ingratitude. One sage cynically said, "No good deed goes unpunished."

Contrary to these statements, the teaching of God's word is "whatever good anyone does, this he will receive back from the Lord ..." (Ephesians 6:8 ESV)

Regardless of the response of others to any good thing you do, whether negative or positive, the response you should be concerned about is the one from the Lord. When you do good things for others even if they do not deserve it, your reward is in knowing that God will bless you for it.

In fact, this is exactly what Jesus taught us. "And if you give even a cup of cold water to one of the least of my followers, you will surely be rewarded." (Matthew 10:42 NLT)

The purpose in doing good for others is to honor the Lord of our salvation. He spent His life doing good to others (Acts 10:38) and He set the example for us to do the same thing.

Did you know that what we call the "Golden Rule" is a direct statement of Jesus? He said, "Just as you want men to do to you, you also do to them likewise." (Luke 6:31 NKJV) We have paraphrased it to say, "Do unto others as you would have others do unto you."

Do not wait for others to act favorably toward you. Bless them first!

Fill your day with good deeds done for others. You will find such deeds will provide their own reward for you. Even so, remember that the Lord has promised much more for you in eternal rewards.

We are not doing good deeds to earn salvation. That is absolutely, totally received only by faith. However, we are to glorify our heavenly Father by the good things we do in the name of Jesus. "Let your light so shine before men, that they may see your good works, and glorify your Father which is in heaven." (Matthew 5:16 KJV)

Let today be a day when you show the blessings of the Lord to others through your own works expressing His love. Remember, no matter what the world's philosophy about good deeds done for others, the promise of God's word for you is that He will return blessings to you for every good thing you do for someone else. (Ephesians 6:8)

Reasons To Stop Going To Church

Most people who do not regularly attend church services believe they have good reasons. I have heard most of the reasons (or excuses) as you probably have. A movement today teaches against involvement with the organized churches. However, here are some of the most frequent among the many I have heard.

"I'm tired after a long week's work." A warm spirit of worship can be as restful and refreshing as a short vacation. It is a chance to get away from the intense pressure of the workplace and get your mind on the restorative presence of the Lord. Another answer to this excuse is that your attendance declares your gratitude to God for your health and ability to perform a job. It also states you are thankful to have one!

"There are hypocrites there." Although a flippant answer would be, "Come on in—there is always room for one more," the legitimate answer is that every corporate body is made up of people who are striving toward the fullness of God. Churches should be places of healing, spiritual growth, and finding answers. None of us is perfect including you and me. If you look at the lives of others as your guide or standard, you will miss your highest opportunity. Churches will always be imperfect because imperfect people populate them. You go to church looking to Jesus not other people.

"I can worship anywhere." It is true. You can worship God anywhere. However, that is not a legitimate reason for not attending church. You should worship at times other than when in a church service. Corporate worship or the gathering of Christ's body for worship has a distinct and valuable place in the life of the believer. Fellowship strengthens faith and the believers. That is why the Scripture admonishes us "not to neglect to meet together." (Hebrews 10:25)

"They want your money." The Apostle Paul was accused of pursuing money. He answered his critics by saying that he was not after anyone's gift to him. Rather he wanted to teach others to give to the work of God because of the blessing they would receive for their giving.

"I have more important things to do." This is interesting. To use this excuse you must devalue the union of believers and their corporate testimony. This viewpoint determines whether your attendance is always, sometimes, or never.

Does it matter where you attend church services? I hope you know that it definitely does! Do you have an excuse for not being in the house of God with His people on the Lord's Day? Look at your reasons with honesty and decide if your priorities are in order.

Feeling Trapped?

Have you ever felt trapped? Is that your condition right now? If it is, I have an answer for you.

The Psalmist said the Lord, "will release my feet from the snare." (Psalm 25:15 NIV) A snare is a trap set by a hunter to catch an animal. It is also a trap set by Satan, the enemy of your life, to capture you.

Life is full of these snares set in our path by the one the Bible calls our adversary. You are walking through life on a path that has snares and the only way you will avoid them is to be spiritually diligent constantly seeking to walk in the Lord's way.

Whatever circumstance or sin has you enslaved right now, the Lord has promised to set you free if you will put your trust in Him.

Additions may have you trapped. Your snare may be an ungodly involvement with another person. It may be your willingness to be deviously disloyal to your friends. Satan's snares take many forms.

Whatever is holding you hostage today can be a trap set by the enemy of your life to keep you from serving God and fulfilling the plan He has for you.

Here is the good news. Christ will set you free if you will totally trust Him. "Then you will know the truth, and the truth will set you free." (John 8:32 NIV)

If you have not avoided the snares set by Satan to trap you, there is an answer. It is not too late for you. You can be the person your Savior wants you to be.

This page started with a promise. The Lord *"will release my feet from the snare."*

Whatever has ensnared you … entangled you … trapped you … captured you … is a bondage that will be broken by Christ who gives us liberty by faith in Him.

I submit to you today that Christ is Truth; He is freedom; He is victory. Moreover, He is for you! He will give you release today when you put your faith completely in Him.

Encountering God

There is a time, we know not when,
A place, we know not where,
That marks the destiny of men
To glory or despair.
    -"Beware! O Soul, Beware!" by J. A. Alexander

God has a meeting planned with you. He will encounter you at some point in time—at some planned place. In that time and place you will have the opportunity to make a decision that will impact your life for as long as you live.

This "time of destiny" is illustrated several times in the ministry of Jesus. He encountered the unnamed woman at the well of Samaria. It is very interesting that Jesus decided to travel through Samaria that day. Jews usually avoided Samaria and even if it made a trip longer, they detoured around it.

The meeting with the woman of Samaria changed her life forever. It also changed the whole village where she lived. It was because the meeting, unexpected but planned by God, between this woman and Jesus was a divine encounter. She could have rejected Jesus but she chose to accept Him. It is a fascinating story. Read it in the fourth chapter of the Gospel of John.

Another example of a divine encounter was the meeting between Jesus and the young man, described as a "ruler" and "very rich." This meeting ended in sadness for the man because he was unwilling to accept the offer of Jesus of eternal life! He made the wrong decision. It is in chapter 18 of the Gospel of Luke.

When that divinely planned meeting comes to you, make the right decision—and such a time will come for you. It will seem like an ordinary event or circumstance of the day. You will have the opportunity to make a decision that will change your life. Sometimes it will require a "Yes" and sometimes it will require a "No."

In that moment, make the decision that honors God and it will be the right one!

A Powerful Gospel

The Gospel of Jesus is a message of power. Some consider the Christian message to be a philosophy. Some identify it as a call to high ethics. Teaching that is more modern might call it "how to live your best life now."

In fact, the Gospel is power. John's Gospel record tells us that the very people Jesus came to save rejected Him. However, to those who received Him, "to them he gave the power to become the sons of God, even to them that believe on his name." (John 1:12 KJV)

The Gospel is the very power of God—power to receive a new life; power to change; power to get up when life has put you down; power to endure and triumph; power to use the sword of the Spirit; power to hold the shield of faith; power to live the life Christ has called you to live!

Paul, the great apostle, spoke clearly of His calling when he wrote the Corinthians. He declared that the Lord did not send him to them with eloquent words of man's wisdom. Paul clearly explained he had been sent to preach the power of Christ. He said, "The message of the cross is foolish to those who are headed for destruction! But we who are being saved know it is the very power of God." (1 Corinthians 1:18 NLT)

The Gospel is "good news." It is not just good news about God's power—it is God's power! The Gospel is great teaching about life. However, beyond that it is the power to live that good and victorious life.

In Christ, we have power to prevail. "The weapons of our warfare are not of the flesh but have divine power to destroy strongholds." (2 Corinthians 10:4 ESV)

The Christ life is lived in Christ's power. Otherwise, it is just an exercise of futile weakness.

The Gospel is not education—not words and talk—not reason and learning; it is the power of God!

"For the kingdom of God is not a matter of talk but of power." (1 Corinthians 4:20 NIV)

Great Forgiveness

As Jesus was dying on the cross, He spoke seven times. Someone has called them His "famous last words." They were not actually His last words, but they were the last words He spoke before His death and resurrection.

The first thing He said was, "Father, forgive them for they do not know what they are doing." It was a prayer for those who were responsible for crucifying Him.

How totally like Jesus these words were. They were a prayer for others. In His time of greatest anguish, His first thoughts were for others.

He asked for forgiveness for the guilty. When Jesus told Pilate that he could have no power over him unless His Father had granted it, he said that those who delivered him to Pilate had the greater responsibility. Therefore, those who arrested Him had a great guilt.

However, Jesus chose the way of love. Not only was He asking for their forgiveness by the Father, He was forgiving them.

His whole life was about forgiving others and now at His death, He stays true to His own teaching.

Christ is the purest exemplification of His own teaching. In this, He is again a perfect example for us. He had said, "I say to you, Love your enemies and pray for those who persecute you." (Matthew 5:44 ESV)

What an example of love and forgiveness He is for us. In the most difficult time of His sojourn on earth, He practices forgiveness.

How important it is that these were the first of His last words!

If Jesus could forgive the traitors and murderers who had put Him there, can we accept the grace He provides us and forgive anyone who has wronged us? Surely, no one has committed an offense against you that is comparable to the sins that Jesus forgave.

When Stephen, the first martyr for Jesus, died as enemies of His Savior stoned him, he prayed, "Lord, do not hold this sin against them." (Acts 7:60 ESV)

Stephen followed Jesus in forgiving. Let us by God's grace do the same.

He is Risen

Easter is a time of hope and renewal.

Christians everywhere celebrate the resurrection of Jesus Christ at Easter. Think about that supernatural foundation for faith in Christ. It is the ultimate necessity for validating your faith as a Christian believer. In other words, if you do not believe Jesus literally rose from the dead, you do not have the faith required to be a Christian.

Paul the apostle wrote, "And if Christ be not risen, then is our preaching vain, and your faith is also vain." (1 Corinthians 15:14 KJV) It is not only true that Jesus rose from the dead—we must *believe* that He did!

This is not a "Christian" myth. It is not a "Christian" allegory. It is not a "Christian" feel good fable. Some—even some who purportedly preach and teach the Christian faith—would have you believe that the resurrection is symbolism. That is in direct contradiction to the message of faith and trust in Christ that the Apostle Paul taught. He said, "And if Christ has not been raised, your faith is futile; you are still in your sins." (1 Corinthians 15:17 KJV)

Christ's resurrection guarantees eternal life to the believer. If death had conquered Him, we would have no hope of eternal life. However, because Christ rose from the dead and in doing so conquered death forever, the Christian believer lives knowing that he has eternal life.

The resurrection of Jesus makes it possible for us to live without fear of dying! His resurrection assures us that we have eternal life and death is only a transition from earth to heaven.

"The last enemy to be destroyed is death." (1 Corinthians 15:26 NIV)

"O death, where is your sting? O grave, where is your victory? Thanks *be* to God, who gives us the victory through our Lord Jesus Christ (by His resurrection)." (1 Corinthians 15:55, 57 NKJV)

Because He lives, we shall also live forever!

April – May – June

The Two Greatest Days in History (1)

Although many will disagree that the two greatest days in the world's history are the day of the crucifixion and the day of the resurrection, the Bible assures me that they are the two greatest of all days.

The day Jesus died on the cross was the fulfillment of God's plan from the foundation of the world. (Revelation 13:8) The Father had planned the salvation of mankind before time began.

To think that one man could die for the sins of all men is a powerful concept. It is the heart of the Gospel of Jesus.

"For as by the one man's disobedience many were made sinners, so by the one man's obedience many will be made righteous." (Romans 5:19 NRSV)

The Cross declares that:

1. Sinful man needed a Savior.
2. Jesus, the sinless Son of God, qualified as the Savior.
3. Jesus willingly and obediently died giving His life to redeem us from sin.
4. God's justice was satisfied by the "Lamb of God who takes away the sin of the world."

The Father surrounded Calvary with six miracles on the day of the crucifixion. It was another way that God validated the sacrifice of Jesus on the Cross.

For us individually the most wonderful part of the message of the Cross is that Jesus died for you and me. That is what the Apostle meant when he wrote to the Romans, "God showed his great love for us by sending Christ to die for us while we were still sinners." (Romans 5:8 NLT)

Yes, Jesus died for all the people of the world. Included in that truth is the fact that His sacrifice of Himself was also an expression of His personal love for you and me.

The day of Jesus' crucifixion was one of the two greatest days in history. The other greatest day was the third day after He died on the Cross.

The Two Greatest Days in History (2)

I recently wrote about the two greatest days in history. One of those days was the day of Jesus' crucifixion. The other was the third day after the crucifixion when Jesus walked out of the tomb.

The events of these two days have powerfully impacted the world. Because Jesus died and rose from death, every individual can have the assurance of eternal life.

The message of the Christian Gospel is Jesus. He died on the cross. He rose from the dead. He lives forever.

By faith in Him, we share His victory over death and His eternal life.

The sacrifice of Jesus on the cross was vicarious (He died for us); it was voluntary (He obediently and willingly gave His life as the final sacrifice for sin); it was victorious (He fulfilled the purpose and plan of the Father).

His resurrection from the grave was the seal on His victory. He walked out of the tomb alive, eternally giving us the assurance that we can live forever with Him.

His resurrection guarantees our faith. "Because I live, you will live also" Jesus said. (John 14:19)

His resurrection conquers mankind's greatest fear. He defeats death so our fear of death is defeated in Him. Paul said it for us. "O death, where is your victory? O death, where is your sting?" (1 Corinthians 15:55 NIV)

You can live your life in spiritual victory because He lives! At the end of life in this world, you can crossover from this world to eternity without fear because His resurrection conquers the fear of death. Read 1 Corinthians 15:55 again! It is true!

"Because He lives I can face tomorrow
Because He lives all fear is gone
Because I know He holds the future
And life is worth the living just because He lives."
- "Because He Lives" by Bill and Gloria Gaither

He Is Alive!

Our risen Lord appeared to His disciples numerous times after His resurrection. His purpose was to establish the testimony of His resurrection forever. The Bible expresses His resurrection as guaranteed by "many infallible proofs." These are the appearances the Bible records:

1. To Mary Magdalene alone at the tomb. (John 20:11-18)
2. To certain women as they were leaving the tomb. (Matthew 28:1-10)
3. To Simon Peter alone on the day of the resurrection. (Luke 24:34)
4. To the two disciples on the way to Emmaus on the day of resurrection. (Luke 24:13-35)
5. To the ten disciples (with Thomas absent) and others with them. (John 20:19-24)
6. To the disciples again (with Thomas present) at Jerusalem. (John 20:26-28)
7. To the disciples when fishing at the Sea of Galilee. (John 21:1-23)
8. To the apostles and more than 500 brethren at the time of the ascension. They accompanied him from Jerusalem to Mount Olivet, and there they saw him ascend "till a cloud received him out of their sight." (Mark 16:19; Luke 24:50-52; Acts 1:4-10)

9. To James, although we do not know details. (1 Corinthians 15:7)

10. To Paul near Damascus. (Acts 9:3-9, 17; 1 Corinthians 15:8; 9:1)

11. Luke's words implied there were other appearances of which we have no record. (Acts 1:3)

These disciples knew He died. That was indisputable. It took miraculous certainty to assure them that He was alive again! They were convinced He was dead. They had to be convinced He was now alive!

He saw them face to face. They touched him. (Matthew 28:9; Luke 24:39; John 20:27) He ate bread with them. (Luke 24:42-43; John 21:12-13)

They doubted so we would not have to doubt. They were convinced so we can be convinced.

He is alive.

Appointment

Early, on the first day of the week, Mary Magdalene and some other women went to the tomb where they had laid Jesus after His crucifixion. They were there to anoint His body with spices.

Instead of finding the body of Jesus, they saw an angel. The angel told them that Jesus had risen from the dead and he gave them a message from the Lord. The angel gave them this message from Jesus: "Tell my disciples and Peter to meet me in Galilee." (This is recorded in Mark chapter 6.)

The only one He named individually was Peter. This same man had denied Him three times. After his third denial, Peter went out and "wept bitterly" at the realization of what he had done. All the Apostles had forsaken Him as they fled when He was arrested. However, Peter's denial was worse—it was deeply personal. It was the worst thing he had ever done. He had sinned against his Savior.

Jesus wanted Peter to know that He forgave him. That is why He named Peter and specified that Peter had an appointment with Him in Galilee.

Jesus did not forget him, and He forgave him.

He will never forget you—and He will forgive you!

Your failures are not your future. You have an appointment with the Lord. It is an appointment that He has made with you.

Peter had to do something to keep his appointment with Jesus. He had to go to Galilee because that is where Jesus said He would meet Him.

You will have to do something to keep your appointment with Him. Hear Him! He is calling your name and telling you where to meet Him. Go to the "Galilee" of your appointment and meet Him. When Peter obeyed Him, it changed his life. Keeping your appointment with Him will change your life, too.

The Neighbor

One of the greatest parables Jesus told was "The Good Samaritan." He told it when a man asked him the question, "Who is my neighbor?" I see at least three powerful truths that stand out in this parable.

What's yours is mine; I will take it!

Jesus told the story of a traveler who was on his way from Jerusalem to Jericho. Thieves attacked him, beat him, and stole all he had.

This is a major tenet of the world philosophy. It is a play on the old canard "might makes right."

When a person's possessions are wrongfully taken by force, deception, or coercion of any kind, the taker is like the robbers in Jesus' story. It is the way of the world for the strong to take from the weak.

What's mine is mine; I will keep it!

A priest saw the injured man and crossed the street to avoid him as he walked past. Another religious leader, a Levite, did the same thing. Jesus is saying that religion is not the answer for man's needs.

Selfishness is a curse that only love can cure. The people that you would expect to show love and compassion to the victim—religious leaders—failed miserably as they decided to keep all they had instead of helping the man who was in great need.

What's mine is yours; I will give it!

A man came along the road and saw the injured man lying there in need. He stopped and helped him. After attending his wounds, the helper took the man to a safe place. He paid his bill in advance and told the innkeeper to take care of him. He assured the innkeeper that he would return to pay any additional charges incurred for the man's care.

You can only keep what you are willing to give away. Jesus told the young man who was seeking eternal life to give up everything for Him and he would have treasures in heaven. And he warned all of us against the selfish hoarding of the world's goods when He said, "Store your treasures in heaven ..." (Matthew 6:19-21)

On The Edge

In the early days when public travel in the west was largely by stagecoach, a company was looking for a new driver. He would be the primary driver for one of the company's most important routes.

The transportation company decided to ask one question in the interview process to choose their new driver.

The question was, "If you were driving on a high mountain road and driving off the edge of the road meant a long fall to tragic death, how close could you drive to the edge of the road without dropping off?"

Each prospective driver touted his ability. One said he could drive within inches of the edge without falling. Another said he had driven within one inch of the edge without falling. Still another said he had actually driven so close to the edge of such a road that one-half of the wheel was over the edge without the stagecoach falling off the cliff. The competition for the new driver's job was stiff.

The final person interviewing for the job was asked the same question. His reply was, "I do not know. In my coach driving experience, I have always tried to see how far I could stay away from such an edge." He won the job!

Some people want to live as close to spiritual danger as they can. When you live too close to the spiritual dangers in life, the problem is that you may fall into that spiritual abyss that endangers your spiritual life.

Never try to see how close you can walk to the path of sin in the world. Make it your goal to stay as far away from sin and attractions of the world system as you possibly can. The farther you are from such dangers, the less likely it is that you could be sucked into that life failure.

Live as close as you can to God. That will keep you from living too close to the edge of sin and failure.

This Day For You

"This is the day that the Lord has made." (Psalm 118:24 NKJV)

What day is this? What day is that special day that the Lord has made?

It is this day. It is whatever day you are reading this chapter. Every day is God's chosen day for you. Every day is a special day that He has planned for you. So if you are waiting for a certain day for God to shower His blessings upon you, wait no longer. This is His day that He has given to you!

If you need salvation in Christ, this is the day He is ready to receive you. "I tell you, now is the time of God's favor, now is the day of salvation." (2 Corinthians 6:2 NIV) This is a day appointed for you. It is a day of His favor for you. The day of favor is a day of salvation.

Does it mean there will never be another day for you to come into Christ? I hope not. However, it does mean there will never be a better day for it! Every day of delay is a day wasted.

We said, "This is the day the Lord has made." I could accurately carry that further and say it is the day He has made for you.

There is a time, there is a place, and there is a day of His choice. The Word says that day is today! Do not let the hours of this chosen day that the Lord has made for you slip away into the night without your finding and feeling the touch of His hand on your life!

William P. Register, Sr.

How many days have you breathed air in this world? You can easily calculate that number with Internet assistance. However, the number of the days of your life that have fallen into the tomb of the past is not the important number. The important number is "one!" That is the number of today. One day is today.

Moreover, this is the day that the Lord has made for you!

More

The story goes that someone once asked John D. Rockefeller how much money he wanted. He reportedly replied, "Just a little more."

The rich farmer that Jesus spoke of in Luke chapter 12, decided to tear down his barns and build more space for his harvests. He did that so that he could keep more of his wealth. Jesus said, "Tonight your soul will be required of you."

Jesus made it clear. He said, "One's life does not consist in the abundance of his possessions."

Jesus' statement was a direct contradiction of the world's philosophy. Our earth anchored belief is that the more one owns the more successful he is, the happier he is, and the more he is to be admire and envied.

If you spend your life seeking more of the world's rewards, you are pursuing the wrong goals. Just as chasing the wrong things will accumulate more of the wrong things, seeking the right things will accumulate more of the right things.

Jesus did state that He wants us to have more of the right things. The Amplified Version of the Bible puts His words like this: "I came that they may have *and* enjoy life, and have it in abundance (to the full, till it overflows)." (John 10:10)

> More about Jesus let me learn,
> More of His holy will discern;

Spirit of God, my teacher be,

Showing the things of Christ to me.

– "More About Jesus" by Eliza Hewitt

Make sure your pursuit for more includes seeking more of Jesus. Following Him and His teaching will build your life on the right foundation. It will accumulate the right treasure and secure it in the right place.

Lay up for yourself treasures of heaven and you will have treasures in heaven.

A New You

Jesus makes you a great offer. He offers to trade a new life for your old one.

What a deal. The Bible says that though we were dead in trespasses and sins, He has given us life by faith in Christ. (Ephesians 2:1) He will take your old life and give you a new one!

This is the message of the Gospel. Sometimes referred to as being "born again" (John 3), once we have accepted God's offer of a "new life," in His sight we become a "new creation." The One who created us, allows us to be created all over again by our faith in the Lord Jesus. "If any man be in Christ, he is a *new creation*: old things are passed away; behold, all things are become *new*." (2 Corinthians 5:17 KJV) The New Living Translation says, "This means that anyone who belongs to Christ has become a new person. The old life is gone; a new life has begun!"

"This is not true for me," you say. It will be if you determine to live a new life by the power of the Spirit whom Jesus gives us to enable us to live (a new life) for Him in this world. " ...the Spirit of truth ... will come to you from the Father and will testify all about me." (John 15:26 NLT)

If you are a believer who has been walking out of fellowship with the Lord, now is the time for you to return to Him and accept the blessings of the new life Jesus has provided for you. Today, if you will live in complete fellowship with Him, He will draw you closer to Himself with every step you take.

"If we walk in the light as He is in the light, we have fellowship with one another, and the blood of Jesus Christ His Son cleanses us from all sin." (1 John 1:7 NKJV)

Today is your day! Plan and purpose right now that you are going to change your walk. Make the decision that you will try to please God in everything you do today and let Him draw you close to Himself.

This is important! Know that walking with God for the fullness of His fellowship will give you a new viewpoint on life. If you are in Christ, you *are* a *new creation.*

"Whoever has my commands and keeps them is the one who loves me. The one who loves me will be loved by my Father, and I too will love them and show myself to them." (John 14:21 NIV)

The Rest of the Story

Several years ago on one of my visits to Belgium, I went to the Lion's Mound monument, which commemorates the Battle of Waterloo. Although now a part of the nation of Belgium, Waterloo was a part of the United Kingdom of the Netherlands when the battle took place.

Waterloo was where Admiral Lord Wellington led a coalition of nations, including his own British troops, into battle against Napoleon and his French army. The battle would determine the future of Great Britain and all of Europe.

On June 15, 1815, the historic battle began. Historians have written of it in minute detail. All of Europe and the United Kingdom knew of the battle. They knew its significance and the consequences of the outcome.

The public waited for news of the ending. There was no means of rapid communication in that era, as it was before telephones or even the telegraph.

When the result of the battle was certain, a ship in the English Channel attempted to inform the homeland as quickly as possible of the results. The ship was sending a signal with the coded flags used in that day to transmit information. The news of the battle traveled from one point to another until all had received the message.

On this occasion, when the signal ship came within range of shore, the message was signaled "Wellington Defeated ..." Right at that time a heavy fog came down and the ship could not be seen. The news spread from station to station across England, "Wellington Defeated." There was depressing gloom throughout the country. Their hero and greatest military leader had been defeated! What consequences for their nation and the Continent would ensue?

After a few hours, the fog lifted. The signal resumed and was delivered in its entirety: "Wellington Defeated ... Napoleon!" England rejoiced after receiving the complete message and eventually all Europe rejoiced in the triumph of freedom.

The cross seemed to be a defeat for the Son of God. All of His followers believed it was. All they knew at that point was "Jesus defeated ..." However, on the morning of the third day, the complete message came through. He came out of the tomb with the triumphant declaration, "Jesus defeated Death, Hell, and the Grave!"

Now His victory is your victory! Accept it by faith today.

The Cross

It has been said, "Next to the cross, light is the most beautiful symbol of the Christian life and experience." However, the cross and light are really one.

Calvary is God's blazing beacon, lighting up the dark coasts of our lives. That beacon, like a lighthouse warning of dangerous shoals, keeps us from life-destroying dangers if we give attention to it.

> In the cross of Christ I glory,
> Towering o'er the wrecks of time;
> All the light of sacred story
> Gathers around its head sublime.
>
> When the sun of bliss is beaming
> Light and love upon my way;
> From the cross the radiance streaming
> Adds new luster to the day.
> - "In the Cross of Christ I Glory" by John Bowring

Supposedly, John Bowring was sailing off the coast of Macao, China, when he saw a burned out church with only the cross still standing. It was from that experience that he wrote this powerful hymn.

Read the words carefully. It speaks of "All the light of sacred story" gathered around the cross. Further, it speaks of the sun "*beaming light* and love upon (our) way." All of this comes from the cross.

The message of this hymn was so much a part of the life of John Bowring that his tombstone bore the title.

Oh, that the message of this great truth would become that much a part of all of us—*above all, a Cross towers over the wrecks of time!*

Its base touches earth telling us that God came near to man. Its arms extend outward telling us that God offers Himself to all men in all places. Its summit points upwards telling us that in Christ, man has a life above and beyond earth's mortality.

Let the Christ of the Cross be the center of your life!

Redeemed

In my church, I recently preached a message I called simply, "Redeemed." Its basis was this Scripture: "You were redeemed ... with the precious blood of Christ." (1 Peter 1:18-19 NIV)

When the word "redeemed" is used in the New Testament, it usually gives the image of one going into the marketplace to buy a slave with the intention of setting him free. You are "bought with a price; you are not your own." (1 Corinthians 6:20, 19 NIV)

Like the words say in the song by the late Ellis J. Crum, "I owed a debt I could not pay; He paid a debt He did not owe."

When you were lost—captured, kidnapped, enslaved—by sin, God sent His son to pay the required price to set you free.

I love the Apostle Paul's words to the Corinthians. "This means that anyone who belongs to Christ has become a new person. The old life is gone; a new life has begun! And all of this is a gift from God, who brought us back to Himself through Christ ... for God was in Christ ... no longer counting people's sins against them." (2 Corinthians 5:17-19 NLT)

You could never have purchased redemption yourself but it is freely afforded you in salvation. The price of your redemption is the sacrifice of the Lord Jesus on the cross. That unparalleled price was the death of His Son taking your place. (2 Corinthians 5:21 NIV)

"Think of it! All sins forgiven, the slate wiped clean, that old arrest warrant canceled and nailed to Christ's cross. He stripped all the spiritual tyrants in the universe of their sham authority ... and marched them naked through the streets." (Colossians 2:14–15 MSG)

Because He has bought your life with the price of His own blood, you are God's property!

Forgiving the Betrayer

Have you ever been betrayed? It is a sinking, discouraging experience.

Betrayal does not come from those who you know are against you. It can only come from those whom you know who should be your supporter—a friend, colleague, defender, family, your church.

An enemy does not betray you. You know and expect he will oppose you. But when a friend or trusted family member turns against you, it is a bitter disappointment.

Who do you think of when you think of "traitor?" Do you think of Benedict Arnold who betrayed his country? Do you think of Judas who betrayed our Savior, or do you think of a name that is personal to you?

If you are thinking of someone who betrayed you, it could indicate that you have not forgiven him. Be sure you have forgiven—or, by the grace of God, forgive him now! If you do not forgive, you are allowing that act of betrayal to continue to impact your life negatively.

More than one person has betrayed me more than one time. However, I'm glad to say I had to pause here for a few minutes to remember those events. They have no affect on my life today. Forgiveness allows you to come to that place!

If you allow betrayal perpetrated against you to affect you today, you are giving that betrayal far more power over you than it should have. In other words, if you have not totally forgiven the traitor, you are allowing his treacherous act to succeed still today! Forgive him—or them—and remove any effect they have on your life today.

You shouldn't allow a traitor to have any power over you today!

A former (or current) spouse, a friend, a church, employer, a pastor, a counselor or therapist, a fiancé – you see how the list of possibilities almost never ends. Whoever has betrayed you is still succeeding against you and will continue to succeed until you have forgiven him.

Take that victory over betrayal today and forgive your betrayer. Then you will become the victor over any traitor and any traitorous act ever committed against you!

He Knows Us

A major shift has occurred in the way you must consider your daily life. Everything you do is subject to documentation that may become public. Many people have learned this to their own chagrin.

Almost everyone has a camera and sound recorder with him or her at all times. There is a camera and recorder in virtually every mobile telephone. Therefore, wherever you are and whatever you are doing or saying can potentially be recorded.

Usually people make recordings because they consider your actions or words to be funny or embarrassing. The record of your behavior can be emailed immediately to anyone, uploaded to public internet sites like YouTube where anyone can access it, and shared with friends on social network places like Facebook.

The ubiquity of cameras and sound recorders has sometimes proven beneficial as when recording wrongful or criminal acts has led to justice.

It has always been true that your words, deeds, and even thoughts are known. There is and there always has been Someone keeping a complete record of our lives.

Some of us react with immediate fear when reminded that God knows us totally. However, it is not His purpose to look for things in us to punish. He knows all about us so that He can watch over us, bless us, and forgive us.

I remember when I was growing up hearing a song called "The All-Seeing Eye." It made me think of condemnation and fearful that God was looking for and keeping a record of every little thing that I did wrong.

Then I discovered Psalm 139 and many other Scriptures like it. I learned that God was watching me in love and for my protection and benefit. The God of Psalm 139 is not a snooping, sinister, ready-to-condemn God. He is a pursuing, eager-to-protect God.

He is not a policeman but a parent! He does not look for things in us to disapprove or condemn but rather things that He can confirm and approve!

Be glad today that your God keeps a record of your life. If you live for Him, He will use the record to bless you now and eternally.

On The Journey

Two men were walking together down a dusty road. As they walked, they discussed issues of great importance to them. They were followers of a new religion and the groups that opposed Him had just killed their leader.

The men could not understand the shocking things that had happened in the last couple of days. Suddenly, their leader had been forcefully arrested, illegally tried, and sentenced to death. The capital sentence had been carried out immediately and now these two followers were trying to understand why it had happened. The unexpected events that had happened so suddenly were the sole topic of their discussion.

No matter how much they tried to answer each other's questions, they were still confused and befuddled by the events that were so graphically real to them.

As they walked and conversed, a stranger joined them. He seemed to appear from nowhere but they welcomed him into their conversation. The stranger asked them about the things they were discussing. They were amazed that he did not already know of the events that had shaken the whole population of their city. However, they told him about the things that had them so disturbed.

The stranger began to speak to them in a way that caused the fog of their confusion to dissipate. Then he went even further and explained to them why those things had to happen.

115

Soon they came to their destination and they invited this stranger to stop with them for food. He agreed and went into their home with them. When they were inside and sat down at their table to eat, a wave of understanding and clarification swept over them.

Suddenly they realized their guest was Jesus whose death by crucifixion they had been discussing. When He allowed them to know it was He, their darkness became immediate light. They then realized that ever since He joined them, they had felt different. "Our hearts were warm within us," they said.

Just because you may not recognize Him does not mean He is not with you. Even though it may not be very clear to you, He is walking with you to lead you into a full recognition of Him. Welcome Him and you will know Him. The more you engage with Him, the more you will realize that He is with you!

Serving Despite Sorrow

In 1871, the tragedy known as "The Great Chicago Fire" virtually destroyed the city. Horatio G. Spafford was a 43-year-old lawyer who lived in a suburb on the north side of the city.

He was married to Anna and they had five children—one son and four daughters. Spafford's real estate investments were lost in the fire and suddenly his entire life savings were gone. That same year, their only son died from scarlet fever, at the age of four.

Two years later the Spafford family took a vacation in Europe. Business delayed Horatio, but his wife and four daughters sailed for their vacation on the *S. S. Ville du Havre*. He planned to join his family in a few days.

In the early hours of November 22, 1873, while gliding smoothly through the waters of the Atlantic, the *Ville de Havre* collided with an iron sailing vessel. Within two hours, the ship sank beneath the waves. Only 47 survived the shipwreck—226 perished. Among those who died were the Spafford's' four daughters. Mrs. Spafford survived. The rescued survivors were taken to Cardiff, Wales. When she arrived, she immediately cabled her husband the message, "Saved alone. What shall I do?"

Spafford immediately left Chicago to join his wife and bring her home. One night on the passage, the ship's captain said to him, "We are passing over the location where the *Ville de Havre* went down." He went to his cabin but was unable to sleep. He prayed, "It is well;

the will of God be done." He soon wrote the words to the wonderful hymn, "It is Well with My Soul."

When peace, like a river, attendeth my way,
When sorrows like sea billows roll;
Whatever my lot, Thou has taught me to say,
It is well, it is well, with my soul.

Though Satan should buffet, though trials should come,
Let this blest assurance control,
That Christ has regarded my helpless estate,
And hath shed His own blood for my soul.

My sin, oh, the bliss of this glorious thought!
My sin, not in part but the whole,
Is nailed to the cross, and I bear it no more,
Praise the Lord, praise the Lord, O my soul!

And Lord, haste the day when my faith shall be sight,
The clouds be rolled back as a scroll;
The trump shall resound, and the Lord shall descend,
Even so, it is well with my soul.

It is well, with my soul,
It is well, with my soul,
It is well, it is well, with my soul.

Horatio and Anna Spafford moved to Jerusalem in 1881 to serve the needs of the people there. They ministered Christ to poor Arabs and Jews, bringing compassion to others from the depths of their own suffering and sorrow.

Creator Love

God's fabulous creation is beyond our human ability to totally comprehend. I have recently been reading again about the magnificence of God's universe. The galaxies that stretch on and on into the unending vastness of the creation, the "black holes" that are still not understood, all of this and much more declares that God has created an expansive universe of immeasurable proportions.

"The heavens declare the glory of God; the skies proclaim the work of his hands." (Psalm 19:1 NIV) That is the way the Psalmist described the unlimited creation in his own limited way.

Certainly there are some who look at the wonders of the universe and can only see a vast result created by reactions within nature over billions of years. I look at the universe and see a magnificent creation by the hand and the word of Almighty God.

The Scripture attributes the whole creation to Jesus Christ, the Lord of glory, with these words in Colossians 1:16-17 ESV. "For by him (Jesus Christ) all things were created, in heaven and on earth, visible and invisible, whether thrones or dominions or rulers or authorities—all things were created through him and for him. And he is before all things, and in him all things hold together."

This point is extremely important. You are not lost in this vast expansive universe and you are not overlooked by the God who created it. You are not just a speck of dust in all of creation's enormity—you are the pinnacle of His creation.

The same Scriptures that declare the wonder of God's creation tell us that He loves us supremely! Jesus came to earth and lived among men and then died the sacrificial death on the Cross to declare this fact. He loves us!

Years ago Stuart Hamblen put this fact in poetic words:

> How big is God, how big and wide is His domain;
> To try to tell these lips can only start.
> He's big enough to rule His mighty universe,
> Yet small enough to live within my heart.

If I Were the Devil

This chapter is adapted from a long ago radio script by the renowned broadcaster Paul Harvey. This was the script of his broadcast on April 3, 1965.

If I were the devil ... I mean, if I were the prince of darkness, I'd want to engulf the whole world in darkness. And I'd have most of its real estate as well as most of its population, but I wouldn't be happy until I had seized the ripest apple on the tree: You.

So I'd set about, however necessary, to take over the United States. I'd subvert the churches first. I'd begin with a campaign of whispers with the wisdom of a serpent. I would whisper to you as I whispered to Eve: do as you please. To the young I would whisper that the Bible is a myth. I would convince them that man created God instead of the other way around. And the old I would teach to pray after me, "Our father which art in Washington ..."

And then I'd get organized. I'd educate authors in how to make lurid literature exciting so that anything else would seem dull or non-interesting. I'd saturate TV with dirtier movies. I'd pedal narcotics to everyone I could. I'd sell alcohol to ladies and gentlemen of distinction: I'd tranquilize the rest with pills.

If I were the devil, I'd soon have families at war with themselves, churches at war with themselves, and nations at war with themselves, until each in its turn was consumed. And with promises of higher ratings, I'd have mesmerizing media fanning the flames.

If I were the devil, I would encourage schools to refine young intellects, but neglect to discipline emotions; just let their emotions run wild. Until before you knew it, you'd have to have armed policemen, drugsniffing dogs and metal detectors at every schoolhouse door.

Within a decade, I'd have prisons overflowing; I'd have judges promoting pornography. Soon I could evict God from the courthouse, then from the schoolhouse, and then from the houses of Congress. And in his own churches I would substitute psychology for religion and deify science. I would lure priests and pastors into misusing boys and girls and church money.

If I were the devil, I'd make the symbol of Easter an egg, and the symbol of Christmas a bottle.

If I were the devil, I'd take from those who have and give to those who wanted until I had killed the incentive of the ambitious.

What'll you bet I couldn't get whole states to promote gambling as the way to get rich. I would caution against extremes and hard work, in patriotism, in moral conduct. I would convince the young that marriage is old fashioned, that swinging is more fun, that what you see on TV is the way to be, and thus I could undress you in public, and I could lure you into bed with diseases for which there is no cure.

In other words, if I were the devil, I'd just keep right on doing what he's doing.

When I Die

The old canard is "nothing is certain but death and taxes." The humorous part of that is supposed to be the play on "taxes." However, the fact is that the one certain thing in life is that you and I will die.

That surely sounds morbid to many people. Someone will ask, "Why do you want to say a terrible thing like that?" Everyone already knows this. Not many want to be reminded of it because they do not want to think about it.

There are good reasons for saying this jolting truth—and it is the truth.

We need to be reminded so we can be prepared for that eventful day. The Bible clearly tells us that after death there is accountability for our lives. The writer to Hebrews called it "judgment." He wrote in the Scriptures "people are destined to die once, and after that to face judgment." (Hebrews 9:27 NIV) God will preside over a judgment that will follow our life on earth.

This is not bad news. It is a glorious statement of God's love. It is not God's desire to punish us! He loves us and wants to reward us!

The reminder that we will meet our God after this life on earth is over should fill us with exciting expectation.

Occasionally I look at the obituary page in the paper. I often notice that there are people of all ages listed. It tells me that any one of us can die at any time. At any age in life, we can be just a step away from death.

The message is, "Be ready always." Knowing that death is certain is no cause for fear. Rather it is an opportunity to prove the great truth of God's word.

"There is no fear in love. But perfect love drives out fear, because fear has to do with punishment. The one who fears is not made perfect in love." (1 John 4:18 NIV)

Death and judgment are not about punishment. They are about victory!!

Scars

The wound heals. The scar never does. Long after the wound has healed, the scar is a reminder of the harm that caused it.

Maybe there is value in scars. Some things we would want to forget are constantly with us because of the reminder of the scars. On the other hand, they can also remind you of things that you should remember. Because you learned something valuable in the hard experience of wounds and hurts that left the scars.

The Apostle Paul, always our guide through the New Testament Scriptures, gave a powerful testimony when he said, "I bear on my body the scars that show I belong to Jesus." (Galatians 6:17 NLT)

Paul had suffered for his faith. His body scars came partly because he was whipped with 39 lashes five times, he was beaten with rods three times, he was stoned once and left for dead, and he endured three shipwrecks. He suffered for his Savior, Jesus.

Paul proudly carried the scars of his suffering and made them a part of his testimony for Christ.

This is not to say that all suffering has positive results, but there are experiences that build our faith and strengthen us in Christ.

Your scars may be from wounds that were not as serious as Paul's were. Regardless of how serious they may seem to others, they were traumatic to you. Your scars should remind you that you came through every wound and attack. Today you are here with the scars but they prove your victory.

When you look at the scars you carry, you can put this title on them: Scars Of Victory.

Is your body scarred? Is your spirit marked? Are your emotions still bearing the reminders of your trauma?

You say, "Yes." And I say you are here! You made it! The attacks scarred you but did not defeat you! So every mark you have from the battles you have fought is a "scar of victory." You are here and you are not defeated.

Friendship

Count your true friends. I mean your *really* true friends. If it takes more than the fingers of one hand to count them, you are greatly blessed. Someone has said, "If you have one true friend you have more than your share."

When I think of true friends, I think of loyalty. A true friend will be loyal to you in every situation. You will never have a greater gift than to have a friend that you can trust at all times. "A friend loves at all times" is a statement in Proverbs 17:17. The NLT version of the Bible translates this as, "A friend is always loyal."

When I think of true friends, I think of truth. A friend will tell you the truth. When he tells you the truth, it will be because he believes it is the best for you.

Many people have said some wonderful things about friends. Another statement in the Bible is, "a real friend sticks closer than a brother." (Proverbs 18:24 NLT)

Another person said, "A true friend never gets in your way unless you happen to be going down."

There is a true friend who is always with you. He is loyal, truthful, and dependable and always there when you need Him.

In fact, He has already given His life for you. "Greater love has no one than this, that someone lay down his life for his friends." (John 15:13 ESV)

You will never have a better friend than Jesus.

"What a friend we have in Jesus. All our sins and griefs to bear!" In 1855, Joseph Scriven wrote those words in a poem that became the great song, "What a Friend We Have in Jesus." I want those words to ring in your heart today. Reassure yourself with the powerful truth—Jesus is your true friend. Keep it your true friend. Keep it in your heart and speak it loudly to yourself today—Jesus is my Friend.

Tests of Our Faith

Maybe you noticed. The name of this book is FAITH WALK. That is exactly what our daily walk with the Lord requires: Faith.

Paul said, "We live by believing, not by seeing" and "The righteous shall live by faith." (2 Corinthians 5:7 NLT & Galatians 3:11 ESV)

It is evident that the Apostle Paul said we couldn't live the committed Christian life guided by the standard of human reason. We can only live the Christian life by faith!

That means in all things we trust Him regardless of what human reason and logic may declare. We know (by faith) that He is leading us whatever the visible circumstances may be.

Even in the midst of greatest hardship and suffering, we stand in our conviction—firm in faith—that God is in control. Nothing can overcome us if we keep our faith in our faithful Lord!

There will be trials of our faith. "Fiery trials" shouldn't surprise us. The tests will come. However, the Apostle Peter says we are to rejoice when those tests fall on us. (1 Peter 4:13)

God's Word is stalwart in declaring His faithfulness to us regardless of the hardship or difficulty we may face. The important thing for us to know is that He is with us whatever the test or trial may be!

"When you go through deep waters, I will be with you.
When you go through rivers of difficulty, you will not drown.
When you walk through the fire of oppression, you will not be burned up;
the flames will not consume you." (Isaiah 43:2 NLT)

No matter what you are going through, our Lord says, "I will go through it with you." By faith, we know it is true!

Servants

Jesus made a very controversial statement. He said, "The greatest among you must be a servant." (Matthew 23:11 NLT) That is directly contrary to the view of the world.

According to Jesus, the path to greatness is the path of service. He lived that life. He is an example to us to live as servants, too.

At Thanksgiving, you will see pictures of some persons in high office standing in the food serving line, serving the poor. However, service is not a photo op.

The servant Jesus was talking about lives a life of serving others. This is not about occasionally performing a good deed. This service is defined by the words that Jesus spoke about Himself. He said, "The Son of Man came not to be served but to serve, and to give his life as a ransom for many." (Matthew 20:28 ESV)

You do not have to be a missionary in a foreign land. You do not have to preach or be a pastor. You do not have to hold a certain position in your church. Being a servant only requires a servant's heart!

The way to true happiness is the way of the servant. When your life is not turned inward with ambitions for your own advancement but when it is turned outward in blessing others, you will find that serving others is the way to gain true satisfaction. That produces true happiness.

God is looking for servants. The goal of the servant is not to become great. Although he may not become great in the eyes of the world, He will be great in the eyes of God and that is the highest accomplishment.

When Jesus said to His disciples that the greatest among them must be a servant, He was telling them how to be great in the kingdom of God. It is not about the world's opinion. It is about God's opinion.

If you want to be highly regarded by the Lord, be a servant!

You Can Make It

If you are dealing with issues today that you do not understand, be assured that you are not alone in that condition. Everyone you meet has things that have happened, are happening or will soon happen in his life that he will not understand.

The wonderful thing is that God knows every issue or problem that you have and He will provide you with the strength to prevail in every situation if you will trust Him.

The Apostle Paul faced many problems. The one that seemed to trouble him most was his "thorn in the flesh." He said he asked God three times to remove it from him but the Lord did not do it. Instead of taking it away, the Lord said to Paul, "My grace is sufficient for you."

Then Paul quoted the words that God gave him which sustained him in dealing with this "thorn." Paul said the Lord told him, "My grace is sufficient for you, for my power is made perfect in weakness." (2 Corinthians 12:9 NIV) From this the Apostle could say, "When I am weak, then I am strong." (2 Corinthians 12:10 NIV)

Paul came to this understanding, as stated in the Amplified version, "When I am weak in human strength, then I am truly strong (able and powerful) in divine strength."

Paul learned the lesson that all of us need to learn. God will bring you through every hardship! It may not be exactly your way, but He will do it in His own way. God allows us to experience our own weakness so that He can reveal His strength. He wants us to depend on His great grace, not on our own ability.

Referring to escape from trials, someone said, "God will pull you through if you can stand the pull." We can stand it because His grace is sufficient for us in all things.

Possessions

A young man came to Jesus with a question. He wanted to know what he had to do to inherit eternal life. When Jesus told him to keep the commandments, the young many replied that he had always kept the commandments. Jesus then said to him, "There is still one thing you must do. Sell all you have and give it to the poor and follow me."

Then the report says that the young man left with great sorrow because he had great wealth. He could not make the decision to give up everything to follow Jesus.

I have always believed that if the young man had sincerely said he was willing to surrender all to follow the Lord, Jesus would have told him it was not necessary to give away everything but it was necessary that he be willing to do it.

This young man did not actually have great possessions—the possessions had him.

Many people believe the Bible says that money is the root of all evil. What it actually says is the root of all kinds of evils is *the love of money.* (1 Timothy 6:10)

The worth of anything you own is determined by the value you assign to it. Moreover, the value you assign to whatever you have determines whether it is a positive or a negative factor in your life.

Anything can be used in the right way or the wrong way. You determine that for everything you have—your car, your home, your money ... an antique, an heirloom, jewelry ... a relationship, a friendship ...

What do you treasure most? That may be the very thing you have to put on the altar first in order to grow in Christ.

> "Do not lay up for yourselves treasures on earth, where moth and rust destroy and where thieves break in and steal, but lay up for yourselves treasures in heaven, where neither moth nor rust destroys and where thieves do not break in and steal. For where your treasure is, there your heart will be also."
>
> (Matthew 6:19-21 ESV)

Suffering and Victory

Annie Johnson was born on Christmas Eve in 1866. When Annie was three years old, her mother died giving birth to her sister. Their father placed them in foster care where they stayed unhappily for about two years. Then a loving Christian couple whose name was Flint adopted them. Annie and her sister took the name Flint and were known as the Flint sister for the rest of their lives.

At the age of eight, she was saved in a revival meeting. Annie Johnson Flint began a life of fellowship with the Lord.

In her teen-age years, Annie learned to express her heart in poetry. When her poetry matured, the verses challenged the mind and moved the heart. Her poems are still among the most powerful declarations of Christian faith.

When her schooling was finished, she began to teach the primary grades in a school near her home so she could attend to her ailing mother.

Arthritis attacked Annie while in her second year of teaching. It became increasingly worse until she was barely able to walk. By the end of her third year, she had to give up her teaching position. For more than forty years, there was scarcely a day when she did not suffer pain.

This is one of Annie Johnson Flint's greatest poetic messages. I will let it speak the message of her heart out of her great suffering.

He Giveth More Grace

He giveth more grace as our burdens grow greater,
He sendeth more strength as our labors increase;
To added afflictions He addeth His mercy,
To multiplied trials, His multiplied peace.

His love has no limits, His grace has no measure,
His power no boundary known unto men;
For out of His infinite riches in Jesus
He giveth, and giveth, and giveth again.

Something is Missing

Today's churches are missing something powerful and wonderful by forsaking the singing of hymns. It is considered contemporary to sing the newer songs in our worship. This is not a complaint about the "new" music, but rather an expression of sorrow because of what we have lost.

There is more Scriptural truth in certain hymns than you will find in a whole collection of newer music.

Just think of the many wonderful truths we hardly ever hear sung.

> Jesus, I my cross have taken
> All to leave and follow Thee;
> Destitute, despised, forsaken,
> Thou from hence my all shall be.
> - "Jesus, I My Cross Have Taken" by Henry Francis Lyte

Great truths in the hymns rise in our thoughts easily, and those strong truths reinforced our faith with their clear teaching.

> There is a fountain filled with blood,
> Drawn from Emmanuel's veins.
> And sinners plunged beneath that flood
> Lose all their guilty stains.
> - "There Is A Fountain Filled With Blood"
> by William Cowper

Great sufferings produced the deep resonance of God's mercy, grace, and love, that so prevail in the teaching of the hymns. Poets such as Fannie Crosby, Horatio Spafford, Annie Johnson Flint, and many others wrote from suffering hearts the beautiful truths that have strengthened us for so long.

> Blessed assurance, Jesus is mine!
> Oh, what a foretaste of glory divine!
> Heir of salvation, purchase of God,
> Born of His Spirit, washed in His blood.
> This is my story, this is my song,
> Praising my Savior all the day long;
> This is my story, this is my song,
> Praising my Savior all the day long.
> – "Blessed Assurance" by Fanny J. Crosby

We may not sing them much in church services now, but I can still sing them "all the day long."

Justice

The bar of God's justice is long and high. He has a "justice system" in place that always provides true justice just as He has promised.

We are in the midst of a high profile, highly publicized criminal trial. It has emphasized the flaws and weaknesses of our legal system. There will always be flaws and failures in a system that depends on men to deny self-interest and do the right thing.

God is just and perfect, so all of His verdicts are right. "Shall not the Judge of all the earth do right?" (Genesis 18:25 KJV) It is a rhetorical question because the answer is obvious. Yes. We can always depend on God to do the right thing.

Everyone will stand before the bar of God's justice to give an account of his life. The Bible makes this very clear. Romans 14:12 says "Each of us will give an account of himself to God. NKJV" And when you stand in that awesome place, you know that God will not be unfair or unjust.

However, that presents this problem. When I look at my life, I know I do not want the verdict that I deserve pronounced on me. I do not want to serve for eternity the sentence that I deserve.

That Great Judge has made a provision for me to receive mercy. I can make the claim that the penalty for my law breaking sinfulness has already been paid. When that claim is proven true, God will show me mercy and forgive my trespasses because He will not require my sins be paid for twice.

"He who did not spare his own Son, but gave him up for us all—how will he not also, along with him, graciously give us all things?" (Romans 8:32 NIV) "God shows his love for us in that while we were still sinners, Christ died for us." (Romans 5:8 ESV)

The judgment for sin laid upon Jesus on the cross satisfied the justice of God. If you accept that provision of Jesus, your sins are forgiven. You can then expect mercy when you stand before God's justice bar because the penalty for your sins has already been paid.

Mrs. Pansy

God has sent some wonderful people into my life. The longer I live, the more I realize this is true, and the more I appreciate the people God sent to be a blessing to me.

One person who was a great blessing to me was Mrs. Pansy. Years ago, I went to a small town in west central Florida to become the Pastor of a new congregation. The only person who was a member of the new congregation at that humble beginning was Mrs. Pansy. She was the organist, church treasurer, and leader of the "congregation." During the years I was there, she was also my biggest supporter.

Although there was no congregation in the beginning, Mrs. Pansy made sure there was enough in the offering to support me. As we began to grow in numbers, she continued to give the same in the church offerings as always. She made it possible for me to have enough income to be able to give all my time to the building of the church. The growth of the church quickly reflected the value of her actions, which made it possible for me to be a full time Pastor.

In my early time at that church, I drove the worst car I have ever owned. There is no need to dwell on that!

Mrs. Pansy knew the constant inconvenience I suffered with that car. A day came when someone in our church traded in a car that was less than two years old with low miles and in very good condition. She came to me and said she wanted me to have it. Shortly afterward, she told me the dealer was ready for me to get the car. I went to get it and everything was arranged for me to drive it back home.

What a blessing she was to me in so many ways. She did it all as service to the Lord.

God has always sent his servant and messenger to me for my need of the hour. Moreover, there are people in my life today who I am sure are assigned by the Lord to advance my ministry and to bless me with their service. I want to appreciate every person that God assigns to me to give me the support I need to serve Him.

Not of This World

Jesus warned us against being a part of this world system. He teaches not to love the world. When He speaks of the world in this sense, He is not talking about the earth. He is referring to a world order, a world system, or philosophy.

This world denies God. The New Testament speaks of it throughout. However, Paul most eloquently expressed it when he wrote these words to the Corinthians:

> "Christ (is) the power of God and the wisdom of God. For
> the foolishness of God is wiser than human wisdom,
> and the weakness of God is stronger than human strength."
> (1 Corinthians 1:24-25 NIV)

God's plan of salvation through Jesus Christ is superior to all the human plans that man has declared. The world system says that salvation through the cross for every person who believes is foolishness. Paul says God's foolishness is better than human wisdom. The message of salvation through Jesus' sacrifice on the cross is weakness and defeat according to the world. Paul says God's weakness is stronger than human strength.

Christians are called to stand against the world's system and order. That is what the Apostle John spoke about when he said:

"Do not love the world or the things in the world. If anyone loves the world, the love of the Father is not in him. For all that is in the world—the desires of the flesh and the desires of the eyes and pride of life—is not from the Father but is from the world. And the world is passing away along with its desires, but whoever does the will of God abides forever."

(1 John 2:15-17 ESV)

In John 17, Jesus prayed that the Father would keep those (us) who have been given to Him, from the world. Someone said the prayer of Jesus was not for the Father to take us out of the world but rather to take the world out of us.

The Mystery of Death

Everyone is going to die. I don't want to be morbid, but it is just a fact. We all know that we are only mortals, so this statement does not surprise anyone. Death is a part of life. The Bible states it clearly. Hebrews 9:27 says every person has an appointment with death.

Since we all face this certainty, let me say some things we all need to know about death.

You do not need to fear death. The reason we do not fear death is that Jesus conquered it when He rose from the tomb.

> "Death is swallowed up in victory.
> O death, where is your victory?
> O death, where is your sting?" (1 Corinthians 15:54-55 ESV)

His resurrection gives us the hope of eternal life with Him. Death is a promotion for those who trust in the victorious sacrifice of our Lord Jesus.

> "Thanks be to God! He gives us the
> victory through our Lord Jesus Christ." (1 Corinthians 15:57)

Death is a transition. The Apostle Paul made it clear. " ...to be absent from the body and to be present with the Lord." (2 Corinthians 5:8 NKJV)

If we are alive at the Second Coming of our Lord, we will be "caught up" in the Rapture. That is a transition from mortal to immortal. The death of the physical body is the same transition.

Death is a promotion. If you read the New Testament as a believer, the fear of the unknown drops out of sight. The Lord provides us with abundant assurances that Heaven is a better place than this earth.

> "No eye has seen, no ear has heard,
> and no mind has imagined
> what God has prepared
> for those who love him." (2 Corinthians 2:9 NLT)

When Will Jesus Come Back?

Maybe people have stopped setting dates for the return of Jesus. No, they haven't. There have always been "date setters" and there still will be. However, Jesus said we do not know the day or the hour that He will return.

Men have always predicted the exact date of His coming. An entire denomination was founded on an erroneous prediction of the time of the Lord's return. They have always been wrong.

In recent years, we have seen highly publicized dates of the Lord's return. False teachers have proclaimed in books, newspaper ads, and other media the time that Jesus would return.

They were all wrong. Every prediction of a date and time that He will return will always be wrong. Because Jesus plainly said that no one knows the time of His coming again. (Mark 13:32)

Anyone who tells you that he knows the time of Jesus' return is speaking contrary to the word of the Lord Himself.

What our Master does want us to know, in all the warnings He gives us about His return, is that we should be ready for it at all times.

"You also must be ready, because the Son of Man will come at an hour when you do not expect him." (Luke 12:40 NIV) This is the real warning about His coming. We do not know a certain day or hour, but we do know that we should be ready to see Him every day and hour.

This is the message Jesus gave about His second coming: Be ready every moment because there will be no advance announcement of His return other than the ones recorded in His written word!

Do you believe Jesus is coming again? If you do not, you will be caught unprepared for the next great event in world history!

Seed and Soil

What quality soil does your life provide for the Word of God to flourish? Jesus taught us that although the seed of His word is generously sown, much of the seed falls on poor soil where it cannot grow.

Read the parable of the Sower in Matthew 13. Jesus says there are various reasons why God's Word does not flourish in every life. In His parable, He makes it clear the seed sown must have fertile, prepared soil to grow and have a successful harvest.

When the explanation of the parable is given to the disciples, it becomes apparent that seed will only grow when it is planted in prepared ground.

The reason seed does not produce a harvest is because some has fallen on the hardened pathway, some on rocky ground without much soil, and some fell where thorns grew. The basic point is the ground is not prepared for the seed.

When His word is sent to us, we must be ready to receive it.

In the metaphor, the soil of our lives that does not allow the word of the Lord to bring a harvest is a shallow life. One failure is giving up when Satan contradicts God's Word and we listen to him. Then, there are those who give up because of persecution or trials. Others are destroyed by cares of the world and deception of riches.

Jesus gave these explanations describing why people hear His Word but do not follow through with a life of victory.

The last category of "life's soil" is the good soil. This person receives the Word, understands its promise and power, and as a result bears good fruit for the Sower. Jesus said that person's life will be abundantly blessed.

You can choose the quality of soil for your life. If you choose for your life to be the good, fertile soil for God's Word in you, the harvest of your life will be unlimited!

"As for what was sown on good soil, this is the one who hears the word and understands it. He indeed bears fruit and yields, in one case a hundredfold ..." (Matthew 13:23 ESV)

The Heavenly Father

It is a wonderful thing to have a heavenly Father. He is someone who is taking care of us in all the aspects of our lives.

The New Testament teaches us that the body of Christ is a family. This means if you have accepted Jesus as your Savior, God the Father becomes your own heavenly Father.

There are promises and benefits offered to those who are children of God by faith.

God the Father answers prayer. Jesus talked about this in Luke chapter 11. He said, "What father among you, if his son asks for a fish, will instead of a fish give him a serpent; or if he asks for an egg, will give him a scorpion? If you then (you earthly fathers) ... know how to give good gifts to your children, how much more will the heavenly Father give the Holy Spirit to those who ask him!" (Luke 11:11-14 ESV)

God the Father faithfully meets all our needs. He desires us to have good things. "Fear not, little flock, for it is your Father's good pleasure to give you the kingdom." (Luke 12:32 ESV) Paul wrote to the church, "Since he did not spare even his own Son but gave him up for us all, won't he also give us everything else?" (Romans 8:32 NLT)

God the Father loves His children. "Those who accept my commandments and obey them are the ones who love me. And because they love me, my Father will love them." (John 14:21 NLT)

The motive that caused God to design His great plan of salvation is described clearly. The sacrificial gift of His Son secured our salvation "because of the great love with which he loved us." (Ephesians 2:4 ESV)

One of the greatest statements in all the Bible is this very simple truth: God is love. (1 John 4:8) And the wonder of it all is, He loves you!

Picking and Choosing

I just came home from grocery shopping. I choose to do most of the shopping because when I go to the grocery store, I shop for the items we need. My wife "buys," I "shop."

When I purchase groceries, I want to get the "buy one, get one free" deal. I want to get the vegetables that are in season and not pay the higher cost of buying them at the "wrong time." I am careful to pick and choose based first on the price.

This may be a good plan when buying groceries. (I'm sure many will disagree with that statement—I know my wife will.) At the least, it will save you some money.

However, this is not a good plan when you look into God's Word. There is no allowance for you to "pick and choose" what you want to accept from His words. In fact, the Bible says of itself, "All Scripture is inspired by God and is useful to teach us what is true and to make us realize what is wrong in our lives. It corrects us when we are wrong and teaches us to do what is right." (2 Timothy 3:16 NLT)

So all Scripture is given by God's inspiration. If any of it is true, all of it is true. No option is given to allow us to choose the parts of His Word that we find acceptable and deny the parts we don't like.

I cannot take God's Word the same way I shop the grocery store! If I accept John 3:16, I must also accept Galatians 6:7, which says, "Do not be deceived: God is not mocked, for whatever (one) sows, that will he also reap." (NKJV)

We have every right to believe in God's love. However, then we must also accept His judgment. Both of these facts are true of God's nature.

Recognize that all the Bible is God's inspired Word and that it is His message to you. It will then become a lamp for your feet and a light on your path. (Psalm 119:105)

When You Pray

Expect that something will happen when you pray. That is faith. When you enter God's presence in prayer, you must "believe that he exists and that he rewards those who earnestly seek him." (Hebrews 11:6 NIV)

The same verse I referenced above also says, "Without faith it is impossible to please God."

"Now faith is confidence in what we hope (pray) for and assurance about what we do not see." (Hebrews 11:1 NIV) We walk by faith not by sight.

So in order to receive anything from God, you must pray and you must believe. We know that is easier said than done!

Faith perseveres. If you have faith, you will not give up on receiving the answer to your prayers. Jesus taught that we "should always pray and never give up." (Luke 18:1 NLT) He taught this principle when He told the parable of the widow and the unjust judge. The whole premise of His teaching was that we should *pray* and *never give up*!

Faith (believing God) will persevere. Giving up before the answer comes is the opposite of true prayer.

I have heard people say that you should only ask once when you pray. This supposition maintains that you need to ask once and only once if you have faith and that if you ask again, it is evidence of unbelief. Jesus did not teach that. He actually taught us to pray until the answer comes.

Today if you are seeking the Lord for an answer in your life, my counsel to you is, keep praying! To have prayers answered by the Lord you must never give up.

Faith is frequently misunderstood. We often think it is a simple formula. Ask, expect, and receive. However, it is really more about staying the course.

Faith makes things possible—it does not make them easy.

Overflowing Blessings

In the best known of all the Psalms, the 23rd, the writer says, "My cup runneth over." In the NLT version, it is stated this way: "My cup overflows with blessings."

Overflow speaks of the abundance of His blessings. They are overflowing every "container" we have in our lives. We do not have enough room to contain all the favor that our Lord showers upon us.

One of the greatest reasons God pours blessings upon us is for us to be able to bless others. God blesses us so we can share with others.

The more we give to others the more room we have for God to continue to pour His blessings on us. In other words, if you keep all that God provides for you there will be no room for the Lord to give you more!

If we keep all God gives us, the content of our "cup" becomes stagnant. When we overflow, all those around us are blessed.

God blesses us so we can bless others. Our desire for the blessings of God should be so we can share the blessings. The more we give the more God gives to us. That's why God gives us an overflow.

> Fill my cup, Lord, I lift it up, Lord!
> Come and quench this thirsting of my soul;
> Bread of heaven, feed me till I want no more--
> Fill my cup, fill it up and make me whole!
> - "Fill My Cup, Lord" by Richard Blanchard

Fill my cup, Lord, so I will have blessings to distribute to others. My desire to receive is so that I can give!

The more God fills your cup, the more you can do for God. If there is an overflow in your own life, you have abundance to share and bless others. The more you give to others, the more God will give to you. (Luke 6:38)

Authority

Jesus was different from other teachers. The Scriptures tell us that one of the main things the people said about Jesus was that He spoke as one who had authority and not as the other teachers.

We have authority that comes from Him. Jesus repeatedly told His disciples that they had authority to speak in His name. If we are His disciples then the promises He made to His disciples are promises made to us. That gives us the authority of His name.

Six times in three chapters of the Gospel according to John, Jesus gives His disciples the authority of His name. (John 14, 15 & 16) He tells us that we are to ask and believe as we pray in His name.

Authority is not autonomy. We have nothing apart from Him and without Him we can do nothing. Jesus said that. "Without me you can do nothing." (John 15:5 NKJV) Therefore, this authority given to us does not give us the ability to stand alone in any power of our own—it gives the right to depend totally on Him.

Jesus said, "All authority in heaven and on earth has been given to me. Go therefore and make disciples of all nations ..." (Matthew 28:18-19 ESV) We are to go forward in His authority—in His name—to serve Him.

It is an awesome and challenging concept. Jesus gives us the authority of His name! What a challenge!

Because of His name, we can now approach the Father. We come to the throne of God's grace " ...fearlessly and confidently and boldly ..." because of the power of His name. (Hebrews 4:16 AMP)

Kittie L. Suffield said in her song, "Little Is Much If God Is In It:"

"There's a crown—and you can win it,
If you go in Jesus' Name."

"There is no other Name ...!" (Acts 4:12 NIV)

July – August – September

Service or Servitude?

Service or servitude? There is a big difference.

Service is what you choose to offer others. Servitude is the condition of having to serve or obey another person. Service is freely given; servitude is a requirement.

Jesus taught us to serve others in every way and to do it willingly. For example, He said if you are required to carry another's load for a mile, do not stop there. Go beyond requirements and gladly carry the load a second mile.

Servitude puts a burden of compliance upon us. It leaves no options or choices.

However, serving others in obedience to the Lord means we are really serving Him. We do it because we choose to do it. There is great joy in truly serving others freely.

Recently I spent a week in the Great Smokey Mountains as a guest of individuals who offer this retreat to ministers and missionaries as a gift. It is a calling God has put on their hearts to serve those called to serve continuously. It is such a blessing to have those willing to offer such a sacrificial service!

If you are required to serve others, it may produce no joy unless you do it with a true desire to serve. If you serve by your own choice, the reward is joy and satisfaction.

We have the choice to follow the teaching of Jesus and serve others. He said this is the path to true greatness. The world may not recognize it, but servants are accorded the highest level of greatness in the Kingdom of God.

Serving others is definitely a choice. "But he that is greatest among you shall be your servant," is what Jesus said. (Matthew 23:11 ASV) When you believe the true reward of serving others, it is a simple choice. You will gain more by giving than you will ever lose.

A Settled Faith

C. S. Lewis was a great writer declaring Christian truth. His influence lives on in his writings supporting the truth of the Christian faith.

When he was fifteen years old, he became an atheist. About this time, he developed an interest in the occult. There were other strong influences that led him away from God.

However, in later writings he described himself as being paradoxically "very angry with God for not existing."

He had friends who engaged him in serious discussion and debate about the Christian faith. Finally, through a convergence of influences, He became a Christian.

He fought greatly up to the moment of his conversion, noting that he was brought into Christianity like a prodigal, "kicking, struggling, resentful, and darting his eyes in every direction for a chance to escape." So, finally, at age 33 he committed himself to Christ and became one of the Lord's greatest spokesmen.

As a young man, C. S. Lewis embraced atheism and the occult. He then reviewed the claims of Christ and understood that Jesus was his Savior. He was much like the Roman centurion of the Scriptures who looked upon the man on the cross that he had helped crucify and declared, "Truly He was the Son of God."

No matter where you started in your search for truth, God can bring you to a place of absolute faith and make you a spokesman for Him. Wherever you stand right now, God is striving for you to come to Him.

Many people have faced their doubts and questions and have come to the realization that Jesus is Christ. Open your heart to the Lord and He will settle with you all your doubts.

As it was with C. S. Lewis, it may seem that you are in an arduous struggle to come to the place of settled faith. You will arrive at that place, however, if your heart is sincerely open to His truth. You will come to the understanding by faith that Jesus Christ is the Son of God.

Pardon

Pardon is forgiveness. In a legal sense, a pardon granted by the appropriate executive gives the recipient a release from any guilt for a crime committed.

You and I have received a pardon. The cross of Jesus Christ grants us a pardon for our sins.

It is a wonderful merciful act of grace. God, our Father, says to every person who has sinned (that is, all of us), "By grace you are saved through faith. And this is not your own doing; it is the gift of God." (Ephesians 2:8 ESV)

That is pardon for sin and transgressions!

On December 6, 1829, two men, George Wilson and James Porter, robbed a United States mail carrier in Pennsylvania. Subsequently captured and tried, on May 1, 1830, both men were found guilty of six indictments which included robbery of the mail "and putting the life of the driver in jeopardy." On May 27th both George Wilson and James Porter received their sentences: Execution by hanging. The sentences were to be carried out on July 2, 1830.

James Porter was executed on schedule. George Wilson was not. Shortly before the set date for his execution, a number of Wilson's influential friends pleaded for mercy to the President of the United States, Andrew Jackson.

On June 14, 1830, Jackson granted a pardon to Wilson. The charges resulting in the death sentence were completely dropped.

Wilson would have to serve only a prison term of twenty years for his other crimes. But shockingly, George Wilson refused the pardon!

Wilson was returned to court as they attempted to "force" the pardon on him. Record states that George Wilson chose to " ... waive and decline any advantage or protection which might be supposed to arise from the pardon referred to ..."

There was no precedent for such an issue. The case reached the Supreme Court. Chief Justice John Marshall wrote the following in the majority decision: "A pardon is a deed, to the validity of which delivery is essential; and delivery is not completed without acceptance. It may then be rejected by the person to whom it is tendered; and if it be rejected, we have discovered no power in a court to force it on him."

The court ruled that a pardon is worth nothing unless the person to whom it is offered accepts it.

You do not have to accept God's pardon for your sins. He has offered it and you can accept it or reject it. The decision is not God's decision—it is yours. God made His decision for you when His Son died on the cross. By that sacrifice, He pardoned you. You must accept it for it to be effective. You can accept your pardon today. The nail pierced hands of Jesus Christ offer it to you. It is your decision.

All Things

At a low point in his life, Jacob, who became Israel, said, " ...all these things are against me." (Genesis 42:36 KJV) We can all find ourselves in depressing times. That is when we may allow negativity and discouragement to control us.

The Psalmist expresses another viewpoint. He said, "I will cry unto God most high; unto God that performeth all things for me." (Psalm 57:2 ASV)

You can view all things in a positive or a negative way. The power of God comes forth in us when we recognize that He is working in ALL THINGS for our good. (Romans 8:37)

"In **ALL (these) THINGS**, we are more than conquerors through Him. (Romans 8:37 NKJV)

"He who did not spare his own Son but gave him up for us all, how will he not also with him graciously give us **ALL THINGS?"** (Romans 8:32 ESV)

Jesus said, "With man this is impossible; but with God **ALL THINGS** are possible." (Matthew 19:26 NIV)

"Therefore if any man be in Christ, he is a new creation: old things are passed away; behold, **ALL THINGS** are become new." (2 Corinthians 5:17 KJV)

"I can do **ALL THINGS** through Christ who strengthens me." (Philippians 4:13 NKJV)

Let these Scriptures speak to you. The Word tells us where we stand in ALL THINGS, and it is a stance of overcoming and victory.

Then Paul gives us the crowning truth for all the faith that we place in our good God. He says, "And we know that **ALL THINGS** work together for good to them that love God, to them who are the called according to his purpose." (Romans 8:28 NKJV)

We can join Jacob in spiritual depression and believe all things are against us, or we can join the chorus of believers who know by faith that God is putting together a great plan in our lives. That plan puts ALL THINGS together for our blessing from Him.

The Seeker

Jesus told a parable of a shepherd who had a hundred sheep. Looking over the flock, he saw that one of the sheep was missing. Ninety-nine of them were safe in the fold but the shepherd could not ignore the one that was lost.

He left the flock of ninety-nine with others and went out into the wilderness to find the one lost sheep.

This is recorded in Matthew 18 and Luke 15. Those chapters also document other parables of Jesus, emphasizing the same message as the lost sheep.

The point is that Jesus cares deeply about every individual and He will exhaust every avenue to find the one who is lost and bring Him back to God.

Jesus put it this way: "The son of man has come to seek and to save those who are lost."

If you are lost—or have lost your way—Someone is seeking for you. You may not be looking for Him but He is looking for you!

You may think you will embrace Him when you decide to do so. He is seeking you now. *When* you can make the greatest decision of your life, is in His hand and His time.

The seeking Shepherd goes through the wilderness—walks through deep water—battles the weather—deals with every difficulty to bring back the one lost sheep.

"I could ask the darkness to hide me
and the light around me to become night—
but even in darkness I cannot hide from you."
(Psalm 139:11-12 NLT)

That is the picture of the Savior seeking you! And me!

Really Important Things

In 1975, Alabama played football against Notre Dame in the Orange Bowl in Miami. Unlike the outcome of a recent Alabama-Notre Dame national championship game, Notre Dame won the 1975 game by a score of 13-11.

My son, Billy, a young teenager at the time, was at that game. He was brokenhearted that Alabama lost. (I think his only allegiance was "southern roots.") He saw the Alabama coach, Bear Bryant at a book signing the next day in a Miami mall. Billy went up to the coach, and almost tearfully, he said, "Coach, I'm so sorry you lost the game last night." Bear Bryant looked at him and in his low, gravelly voice, said, "Son, it's just another ball game."

Coach Bryant, denied a national championship the previous year by a loss to Notre Dame, came into the 1975 bowl game undefeated with eleven wins. Notre Dame had two losses. Alabama was the favorite to win. Once again, Coach Bryant and his team were denied a championship by the same team.

The next day he could say, "It's just another ball game."

That is having your priorities in order. It is having an understanding that there are important things and there are really important things.

I am not saying those football games had no importance. They were, in fact, important to many people at the time.

Important things may be important at the time. Really important things have lasting importance!

I don't care who any celebrity is dating, or going to marry, or whether they are having a boy or girl. I do care when a friend or family member receives a disturbing medical diagnosis, or a loved one dies, or when a terrible accident disables or impairs someone for life.

I want to be able to distinguish between something that may be important and something that is definitely, *really* important.

God's Time for You

God has planned a time for every person to meet Him. It is a time of His choice. Paul wrote to the Corinthians, "I tell you, now is the time of God's favor, now is the day of salvation." (2 Corinthians 6:2 NIV)

Jesus made it clear. "No one can come to me unless the Father who sent me draws him." (John 6:44 NKJV)

God's chosen time for you will be your time to decide your destiny. This does not mean that there is only one time in a lifetime when you have opportunity to meet God.

If you reject Him and continue to reject Him when He calls, He will finally leave you alone.

This is what J. A. Alexander wrote about in his great old hymn "Beware! O Soul, Beware!" with such powerful meaning:

> There is a time, we know not when,
> A point we know not where,
> That marks the destiny of men
> To glory or despair.
> There is a line by us unseen,
> That crosses every path;
> The hidden boundary between
> God's patience and his wrath.

In one of the saddest verses in the Bible, Jeremiah, the weeping prophet, said, "The harvest is past, the summer is ended, and we are not saved." (Jeremiah 8:20 KJV)

There is a time to meet God, and you must not miss that time. Take the first opportunity the Lord offers you to meet Him. Then you will never have to worry about missing His last opportunity.

The Silver Poodle

When my adult daughter was about 7 or 8 years old, she decided she wanted a silver poodle. Her mother and I were against it, but she continued to ask for the little dog. Over and over she begged for the pet she so desperately wanted.

One day she brought home a story she had written as an assignment in school. She titled it, "The Silver Poodle." It was about a little girl who wanted a silver poodle more than anything in the world, but her parents would not get her one.

It was a sad story and it touched our hearts. Therefore, with a new understanding, my wife and I discussed getting her what she wanted most. The following Saturday, we went out and bought her a beautiful silver poodle.

She named him Pierre. We soon learned that Pierre was a mean dog. He hated children. He was constantly growling, barking, and snapping at everyone in the family except me. By default, I soon became responsible for his care. One day he bit my hand and that was the end of Pierre's welcome in our family.

At various times, as they grew up, my children had pets. Mostly they had dogs. They had big ones and little ones. We remember all of the pets. We still talk fondly about them, and remember how our hearts broke when we lost them. We remember Pierre differently.

Many things in life do not turn out the way we expect. Sometimes the thing you want the most may not be the best thing for you.

You may have a "silver poodle" today. You finally got something you wanted more than anything. You were willing to do anything to have it. You believed it would make you happy. Now you have it and you realize it would have been better if you had never received what you wanted most!

Live to have what God desires for you. He has a good plan for you. Come to the place in your life that you want what God wants for you. Then you will be in joyful contentment.

Truth Always Prevails

My doorbell was ringing. When I opened the door, my new neighbor was standing there. I did not know she was my neighbor but she introduced herself and asked, "Are you the Pastor?" I answered, "Yes, I am."

I had just become the Pastor of a nearby church and had only been in the neighborhood a few days.

The lady said that she was sorry to meet me under the condition that brought her to my house but she had come to tell me about my son. She proceeded to tell me that my son was playing in her backyard, and when she asked him to leave, he became verbally abusive to her.

I said, "That does not sound like something my son would do." I assured her that I would talk with him about her report and that she would quickly receive an apology once I spoke to him about it.

When I found my son and told him what the lady told me, he said, "Daddy, I did not do that!" After talking with him for a few minutes, I decided to take him across the street to see the woman. I believed my ten-year-old son, but I had an adult telling me what she had seen and personally experienced.

We crossed the street and rang the woman's doorbell. When she answered, I said that I had brought my son to speak to her. When she saw him she asked, "Is he your only son?" I said, "Yes, he is." Then she told me that Billy was not the boy who had spoken abusively to her. After some discussion we realized another boy had given her Billy's name when she confronted him.

Things are not always as they seem to be. Sometimes you may think you really know something, but it is not true. This world system has led you to believe a false report. The only answer to deception is truth!

Face the truth in your life with God's Word in your heart. When you do, you will find the Truth always ultimately wins. False accusations, lies, and deception will fall when confronted by truth.

Take Your Cross

Several times Jesus said, "Take up your cross and follow me." Most people seem to identify His statement as a call to a life of suffering, sorrow, and deprivation.

I do not believe that is what He was saying. The connotation of "a cross" causes many of us to think in those negative terms.

To Jesus, the cross was obedience. The Word says, " ...he humbled himself by becoming obedient to the point of death, even death on a cross." (Philippians 2:8 ESV)

To Jesus, the cross was an assignment from the Father. He came to earth to die on the cross. It was the ultimate act of obedience. Obedience speaks of surrender and yielding to the Father's will.

When Jesus challenges us to "take up our cross" and follow Him, He is telling us to daily, and faithfully accept the assignment given to us by the Father—to walk in obedience to His will.

It was important to Jesus for His disciples to understand this. He repeatedly told them that He would suffer, die, and then rise from the dead. They consistently failed to understand or accept that message from Him. He wanted them to understand that His future was the plan of God and that He would walk in obedience to that plan!

He not only told them (and us) to daily take our cross, but He practiced it Himself.

Obedience to Him is not sorrow, suffering, and pain. We do not have to feel physical suffering to "take up our cross" of obedience. We just have to be willing to follow God's plan—His will—daily.

When we obey, we are accepting His assignment for us. Jesus expresses it as us taking up our cross daily and following Him.

Roads to Nowhere

While traveling, have you ever seen a sign telling you that the road ends just ahead of you? That can be very disturbing if you are not expecting it.

With all the information available to us today, that would rarely happen. What is more likely is that you could be going the wrong way on the right road.

Every day I see the signs that warn "Wrong Way" and "Do Not Enter." Yet I frequently see news reports that tell of drivers who have been in terrible accidents because they were driving the wrong direction on the highway or street.

Alternatively, have you ever been driving and knowing you were going the right way? You have a good sense of direction and you just know when you are driving east. Then you see a properly erected sign telling you that you're driving west! Which are you going to believe—your feeling or legally placed information?

This happens every day. There are people who believe they are on the right road but they are not. Some believe they are going the right direction but they are not.

You can be on the Interstate highway thinking you are going the right direction. It certainly feels like you are. Then you see a sign that tells you that you are going in the opposite direction from the direction you thought you were going.

The Bible puts this sign on life's highway: "There is a way that seems right to a man, but its end is the way to death." (Proverbs 14:12 ESV)

You can sincerely believe you are going the right way. Everyone traveling with you can agree that you are going the right way. You could still be going in the wrong direction. If you are, your journey will end at the wrong destination.

Your life is a journey. Make sure you are going in the right direction every day!

Jesus said, "I am the way." (John 14:6 ESV) He is telling us He is the right way!

Is It Good or Bad?

When ownership of automobiles was becoming widespread, many people said it would destroy the family and promote immorality.

There are still many who think the Bible says that money is the root of all evil. (It does not. It says the *love* of money is. 1 Timothy 6:10)

The point is that things are not inherently good or bad. What determines their worth is how you use them.

One of the things that challenges us to make a right decision every day is the use of the Internet. As it is with almost everything else, how you use the Internet determines its worth.

You can use the Internet in detrimental ways or in ways that are beneficial. On the Internet, you can find many helpful and positive things and you can find things that are harmful and morally destructive.

Life is about decisions. You have the opportunity every day to make decisions that will lift you up or tear you down.

For many people, sitting down at their computer brings them that opportunity and challenge.

I am dwelling on computers and the Internet because we need them for productivity in our daily lives, and every time some people sit down at their computers, they are challenged to make a moral decision.

Many situations provide the opportunity to make uplifting value choices but I know of none that occurs more frequently than our use of the ubiquitous Internet. It is not only on our computers but it is on our telephones, iPads, and laptops. That means it is available everywhere all the time.

It is a challenge for many people. Make decisions that edify you and enforce the positive values that God wants instilled in you.

True Happiness

Do you want to be happy? Everyone does. It seems to be the primary goal in life now for most people.

Yet, though everyone seems to be seeking happiness, few really know the way to find it.

Contrary to what many Christians want to believe, Jesus did not come to earth to make us happy. However, a great benefit of knowing and following Him is being able to achieve joy and contentment. That is true happiness.

One day on the Mount of Olives, Jesus taught His disciples the message that we have come to know as The Beatitudes. Nine times that day, Jesus began His statements with the words "Blessed are ..."

The Amplified Bible says that word "blessed" means "happy, to be envied, and spiritually prosperous—with life-joy and satisfaction in God's favor and salvation, regardless of outward conditions." That is real happiness. The Bible's description of happiness as "joy" and "contentment" is much better than our own generally accepted definition of "happiness."

Happiness is from the same word that forms "haphazard." Our happiness is erratic, but true joy is like the water that fills the ocean. The tide is at different levels at various times, but the same water still fills the oceans. The level of the tide has nothing to do with the amount of water in the seas.

Therefore, our joy in the Lord is always full and complete. It may not always seem the same or feel the same but it is always full and complete.

We are told in 1 Peter 1:8 that believing in Jesus fills us with "joy that is inexpressible."

Read Matthew chapter 5. You will find the secret of true joy and contentment. It is a natural (or maybe supernatural) fruit of knowing and following Jesus!

Discipleship

We speak of the early followers of Jesus as disciples—and they were. A disciple is a "learner" or one who is "following to learn."

As followers and learners, you could say that those who were called by Jesus to walk with Him were "following to learn."

Jesus was a teacher. Reasonably then, those who were called by Him were "learners." He said to them, "If you hold to my teaching, you are really my disciples." (John 8:31 NIV)

Discipline and disciple are closely associated words. The discipline of the disciple is to adhere faithfully to the teachings of his Master, or "hold to my teaching," as Jesus said.

Paul tells us we are to discipline ourselves as soldiers, athletes, and farmers. He uses these three examples because each one of them requires a certain dedication or discipline to succeed. Paul is speaking of the dedication that is necessary to be a successful disciple of our Master, the Lord Jesus. (2 Timothy 2:4-6)

The soldier cannot involve himself in civilian pursuits because he is always under the orders of his superior officer. The athlete must train rigorously if he wants to "win the prize." The farmer is subject to the seasons that God created. In each one, there is a discipline to be followed for success.

If we are to succeed as followers or disciples of Jesus, dedication is required. It is "holding to the teachings" of our Lord.

You say you are a Christian. However, are you truly a disciple?

Being a Christian should mean being a "Christ-follower," a "learner" at His feet, an adherent to His teachings through His Word. This is the way to success and victory in your life.

Be a disciple today!

Seed and Harvest

You and I are sowing seed every day. It is not a matter of deciding to do it; we are doing it daily.

Paul the Apostle made it clear that there is both sowing and reaping. The fact is that what we sow determines what we harvest.

"You will always harvest what you plant. Those who live only to satisfy their own sinful nature will harvest decay and death from that sinful nature. But those who live to please the Spirit will harvest everlasting life from the Spirit." (Galatians 6:7-8 NLT)

It is a law of nature that we reap or harvest the same thing we sow or plant. Planting corn produces a harvest of corn.

It's simple. If you want a harvest of good things in your life, plant the right seed. We can plant seed that produces a harvest of "decay and death." Alternatively, we can plant seed that produces a harvest of "everlasting life from the Spirit." The choice is ours.

Paul gives a partial list of the harvest produced by planting the wrong seed: "sexual immorality, impurity and debauchery; idolatry and witchcraft; hatred, discord, jealousy, fits of rage, selfish ambition, dissensions, factions and envy; drunkenness, orgies, and the like." (Galatians 5:18-21 NIV)

He also defines a harvest produced by planting in the Spirit the right seed: "The fruit (harvest) of the Spirit is love, joy, peace, forbearance, kindness, goodness, faithfulness, gentleness and self-control." (Galatians 5:22-23 NIV)

You are sowing seed today, and what seed you sow will determine your harvest tomorrow.

There Is a Time

Someone said, "Timing is everything." By this they usually mean that good things happen when you are in the right place at the right time.

I think this is true, but not in the sense that things just happen coincidentally. I believe good things happen in your life because God has planned good things for you.

"I know the plans I have for you," says the Lord. "They are plans for good and not for disaster, to give you a future and a hope." (Jeremiah 29:11 NLT)

God's word to you is that He has planned good things for your life. This does not mean that you will not have trials, difficulties, and even hardships. It does mean that God's ultimate plan for you is a map that leads you to a blessed destination.

God brings good things to us in His timing. To reap the full blessing He has planned for us in the event or encounter that He has arranged, we must recognize that our "circumstance" is His timing. In other words, we realize—before, during, or after—something that God has done and we declare our praise to Him for the events in which He has put us.

God has put you in the right church. He has given you spiritual fellowship. He brought you in touch with leadership or ministry that enhances spiritual growth. He brought you an enlargement of your business. He has given you ideas and put you with the right person for the right time. They discovered your medical condition early enough for successful treatment. And the list has no end!

If this is being in the right place at the right time, it is because it is the place God put you and He put you there at the right time.

We miss the fullness of the blessing the Lord has planned for us when we do not recognize His hand in the timing of our lives! It is His map and His clock.

Strange Words

Armageddon. Rapture. Tribulation. Millennium. Second Coming.

Although these words have become a part of our vocabularies, we still do not understand a clear meaning of them. They have come to connote a general condition rather than specific event. For example, we have started using "Armageddon" as a general word for any great cataclysmic event. There is even a "new" word has been coined from Armageddon to express a coming explosive event. That word is "Taxaggeddon" which you have recently heard many times on the news.

Nevertheless, these words all have Scriptural meanings and any dilution of them takes away from the important and prophetic power invested in them.

From a Biblical viewpoint, these words point us to remarkable events yet to come. Increased interest in the meaning of these words has intensified because of political and social events happening in the Middle East.

All of the words refer to events that will occur in the plan of God for the future of this earth. And He does have a plan for this world.

The one great thing you need to plan for now is the next event in God's economy. Even if you do not understand the Biblical significance of all or any of these words, you can be prepared for the events they predict.

The first thing you need to do is make sure you are walking with God in salvation, which is the greatest part of His perfect plan for you. Living for Him will prepare you for the Rapture, which I believe, is the next great event to occur. Rapture is the word we use to describe the return of the Lord Jesus to "catch away" His church and take them out of this world.

This "Rapture" is what the angels promised in Acts 1:11 when they said, "This same Jesus ... will come in the same way as you saw Him go into Heaven." It is also explained in 1 Thessalonians 4:13-18. (I strongly encourage you to read this passage!)

When you are ready for His return, you are ready for all the events named in the words on the first line of this chapter. In fact, when you are ready for His return, you are ready for everything else.

The Greatest Gift

Living by the definition of Scriptural love will enrich your life. The best description of love that I have found is in 1 Corinthians 13:4-7 NIV.

> "Love is patient, love is kind. It does not envy, it does not boast, it is not proud. It does not dishonor others, it is not self-seeking, it is not easily angered, it keeps no record of wrongs. Love does not delight in evil but rejoices with the truth. It always protects, always trusts, always hopes, always perseveres."

I believe it requires the love of God in your heart before you can genuinely experience and practice the walk of love toward others. Jesus said, "You shall love the Lord your God with all your heart, and with all your soul, and with all your mind." (Matthew 22:37, Mark 12:30, Luke 10:27 NKJV) When you truly accept the words of Jesus, you can live with true love toward others.

Jesus did not teach an easy way in living the love life and walking the love walk. He said we are to go beyond loving those who love us and treat us well. He said we are to love our enemies and to show good toward those who treat us despicably.

You can do this. Jesus knew it would require our living in close relationship with Him to have the ability to practice His teachings.

That is why His teachings are difficult to practice. Because we cannot do it without Him and that is exactly what He wants. He wants us to depend on Him and know that we must have Him within us before we can practice what He taught us. "Without me you can do nothing," Jesus said. (John 15:5 NKJV)

There is an answer for your relationship with the person who treats you as an enemy, whether a family member, work colleague, neighbor, or just an acquaintance. Perhaps Edwin Markham, the American poet, said it best in his poem, "Outwitted."

> He drew a circle that shut me out–
> Heretic, rebel, a thing to flout.
> But love and I had the wit to win:
> We drew a circle and took him in.

Love—true affection for God and man, growing out of God's love for and in us—is the greatest of all.

You Can't Stop Me

There is no belligerence intended in this title. This is actually about love and forgiveness. Let my message here speak clearly and directly to your heart today.

There are many things you could stop me from doing by either force or persuasion. Some things you cannot stop me from doing, regardless of what you say or do. Because there are some decisions that are entirely mine, and you cannot change them unless I allow you to do so.

First, you cannot stop me from loving you!

Jesus gave us powerful teaching about loving everyone. He gave us especially difficult requirements to love our enemies and to show goodness toward those who treat us wrong! He told us many difficult things but none is more difficult than these are.

Love is a choice. You will need God's grace and His strength to love those who are against you. Jesus said to love even your enemies.

No matter what anyone does to you—says about you—you can still love him. Your loving someone is not his decision—it is yours!

Second, you cannot stop me from praying for you!

I know there are some people for whom you do not want to pray. They do not deserve your praying for them. (No more than you deserve God's grace and forgiveness for yourself.)

However, hear what Jesus said: "I say unto you, Love your enemies, bless them that curse you, do good to them that hate you,

and pray for them which despitefully use you, and persecute you."
(Matthew 5:44 KJV)

What you do for others cannot be based on what they do for you. If you just love those who love you—or pray for those who pray for you—Jesus said anyone could do that! His love for us places strong requirements on us.

It is your decision to pray for anyone. No one can stop you if you are willing to pray for him.

Third, you cannot stop me from going to Heaven.

If you allow the actions of any other person to affect your spiritual decisions, you will make a major mistake. If a friend wants you to join him in doing something wrong, you must make your own decision. It is always your decision whether you will do the right thing or the wrong thing. You decide the course of your life including your final destination for eternity by the choices you make.

There are difficult decisions to make daily. No one else can make your decisions for you. When you want to blame someone else, just remember that no one can keep you from going to Heaven unless you allow it.

No one can ever stop you from doing the right thing! It is your decision!

Uncle Gus

He was not actually my uncle. He was a cousin in the family but I called him "Uncle Gus" because in those days young people always addressed their elders with a title. So, you said "Mr." or "Miss" or if someone was too close for that formality, you called them "Uncle" or "Aunt" or an otherwise appropriate title.

In those days, I never thought about it. He was just always "Uncle Gus."

He was more than a relative. He was a friend, supporter, and encourager.

He was an adult when he gave his life to the Lord and started to serve Him. But once he started, he served the Lord with all his heart and total dedication.

As a young man in high school, I knew the Lord directly called me to preach. When Uncle Gus heard this, he strongly encouraged me to pursue my call from the Lord and to prepare myself to preach the Gospel.

He helped me as I enrolled in the college sponsored by our church denomination.

After my freshman year, and just before I went back to college for my sophomore year, I went to him to discuss a serious issue. I was getting many invitations to preach on weekends but I had no way to get to the churches that invited me.

He told me to find a car that would fit my needs and he would help me. When I found the car I needed, he told me to give him the payment book and he would take care of it. He made the payments on my first car and I used it many times to travel to preaching appointments. That year, I drove to churches in north Georgia, South and North Carolina, and even Kentucky to preach the Gospel.

Uncle Gus gave me my first car. He shared in everything I accomplished for the Lord as I drove that car thousands of miles keeping preaching appointments.

Today I am thankful for his investment in my life and ministry. I write this as a memorial to Uncle Gus.

Persecution

Christians are persecuted in many places throughout the world today. You may think that in this enlightened age the days of persecution for faith have passed. You would be wrong.

In some countries, the government persecutes Christians. In other places, Christians are persecuted by groups that the government allows to operate.

There are still places in our world where Christians are imprisoned, attacked, and even killed for their faith in Christ.

Is our country going in this direction? It may seem unreal to you to contemplate my question. However, I could cite instances that might make one think we have turned in that direction. While we still have a long way to go to reach the point of sanctioned persecution of Christians in America, there are ominous signs.

Consider this one event. A lawsuit filed in Federal court in Texas sought the prohibition of any religious activity at a high school graduation. The Federal judge in this case ruled that there could be nothing mentioned—not a prayer, a Scripture, not even the word "God"—at the graduation exercise. Moreover, he threatened that anyone acting contrary to his ruling would be held in contempt of court and be put in jail.

All this happens under the guise of separation of church and state. But that is not what our Constitution says.

In what direction is our country going? I don't mean economically or politically, I mean in allowing the free exercise of religion—or, more specifically, the Christian faith?

True Greatness

David Livingstone was a great missionary to Africa. Secular historians have emphasized Livingstone as an explorer, but he was really a missionary with God's heart for the lost.

Livingstone returned to his home in Scotland for a time of rest and speaking engagements sixteen years after his first journey into dark Africa. He was asked to speak to the students at the University of Glasgow.

In those days, the undergraduates always heckled the speakers that came. They were going to greet this preacher with every kind of noisemaker. When Livingstone walked to the speaker's podium, his left arm hung limply at his side, having been almost ripped from his body by a huge lion. Innumerable lines furrowed his face, which was a dark leathery brown from sixteen years in the African sun. Bouts of African fever had racked and emaciated his physique. His frail body bore the marks of attacks by jungle savages. Half deaf from rheumatic fever and half blind from other jungle assaults, he stood before them, the missionary/preacher—more than an explorer.

Shocked, the students stared and recognized that here was a man who had burned out his life for God. No noisemakers were heard. There was a hush over the auditorium.

They listened in silence as David Livingstone told about his journeys. He told of the tremendous needs of the vast African population.

"You may ask what sustained me in the midst of these toils, hardships, and incredible loneliness," he said. "It was a promise given me by a gentleman of the most sacred honor.

"It was this promise, 'Lo, I am with you always, even unto the end of the world'." [a]

Livingstone's Savior can be yours, too, if you only ask Him. (John 3:16)

[a]www.asiaharvest.org

Trials and Triumphs

I was recently asked this question: "If the Lord has promised to always be with us, why do we often have to go through such trials and hardships?"

This is the very point of His always being with us. If we never had problems, trials, or hardships, would we realize our need for Him? He told us in His Word that the difficulties we often face will come.

Trials are an expected part of our lives. "Dear friends, do not be surprised at the fiery ordeal that has come on you to test you, as though something strange were happening to you." (1 Peter 4:12 NIV) So expect trials—they will come.

When trials come, He is with you! Jesus promised it when He said, "I am with you always, to the end of the age." (Matthew 28:20 ESV)

The battles in life are spiritual. "For our struggle is not against flesh and blood, but against the rulers, against the authorities, against the powers of this dark world and against the spiritual forces of evil in the heavenly realms." (Ephesians 6:12 NIV)

If you are going to win a battle in the spiritual world, you must fight with spiritual weapons. We have the proper resources to win such battles. "The weapons we fight with are not the weapons of the world. On the contrary, they have divine power to demolish strongholds." (2 Corinthians 10:4 NIV)

There are battles to fight. The battles are spiritual. God has provided spiritual weapons for us to fight these battles. If we fight the battles with God's weapons, we will always be victorious.

Abiding

There is a powerful word in the New Testament that we should understand. It is a favorite word in the writings of the Apostle John who wrote the Gospel account that is named for him, as well as three of the epistles of the New Testament.

That word is "abide." It is used eleven times in the epistles, First, Second and Third John. Strangely, it also occurs eleven times in the Gospel According to John.

The repetition of the word attests to its power and importance. When the reference is to abiding in Christ, it means "living in, with and through Him." When it refers to Jesus and His word abiding in us, it means His word is "alive in us."

Jesus speaks of great power in us when He declares, "If you abide in me (live vitally united to Me) and my words abide in you ..."

The result of that "abiding" is a victorious power of God in our lives!

That state of abiding gives us power to pray. It gives us the power to expect answered prayer. The fact is that when we abide in Him and His words abide in us, He promises us answers to our praying. He states this in language that is powerful and plain. Read John 15:7.

So if you want a direct contact with the Lord which assures He will answer your petitions, be certain that

1. You are abiding in Him (living vitally united to Him).

2. His words are abiding in you.

"Whoever says he abides in him ought to walk *and* conduct himself in the same way in which He walked *and* conducted Himself." (1 John 2:6 AMP)

This is compelling and demanding teaching. It is not for the average person or even the average Christian. But if the deep of your soul cries out for a depth in Jesus that you have never yet found, this is for you!

Signs

Everyone is looking for a sign. This is true for almost every area of our lives.

A girl wants a sign that her fiancé really loves her. The man wants a like sign that he is the center of her affection.

Businesses want a sign that you are a loyal customer. If you take our "red card" (or blue or whatever) we will give you a discount because you have signaled that you are loyal to our store.

Your church wants you to commit to tithe or give consistently as a sign that you are committed. In many of them, you need to prove this to hold any position.

One day some teachers of religious law and Pharisees came to Jesus and said, "Teacher, we want you to show us a miraculous sign to prove your authority." This was after many healings and miracles. They wanted a "miracle on demand" as a sign from Him. (Matthew 12:38-39)

Jesus answered, " ...the only sign I will give (you) is the sign of the prophet Jonah. For as Jonah was in the belly of the great fish for three days and three nights, so will the Son of Man be in the heart of the earth for three days and three nights." (Matthew 12:39-40 NLT)

In these words, Jesus was saying the only sign you will receive is my death and resurrection!

You want a sign that God really loves you. You want a sign that He is aware of you and your needs. You want a sign that He has not forgotten you and that He will never forget you.

You have it. It is His word. In it, He repeatedly declares His immeasurable love for you.

Therefore, here is the sign that God loves you with a supreme and eternal love. Jesus gave His life on the cross for you. He rose from the dead to prove His love can never be conquered—not even by death.

The Water of Life

Water is one of the symbols of the Spirit, power, and presence of the Lord in the Scriptures.

A great example of this symbolism is in the passage that says, "Come, all you who are thirsty, come to the waters." (Isaiah 55:1 NIV)

At the very end of the Bible, here is this grand invitation to all. "Let him that is athirst come. And whosoever will, let him take the water of life freely." (Revelations 22:17 KJV)

When Jesus encountered a woman in Samaria, He addressed her in terms of offering "living water." He was beside Jacob's well and He used her attention to drawing her daily water supply to give her an eternal truth. " ...whoever drinks the water that I give will never thirst," He said. (John 4:14 NIV)

Wanting to never have to return to the well for water, she asked Him to give her this living water. She first applied His words to natural needs when His message was a spiritual one. Once she realized the spiritual impact of His teaching, she spread the word of Him throughout her whole village of Sychar.

Jesus offered her the "water of life" and that is His offer and provision for us today.

Here is His invitation call to us today in the words of Lucy J. Meyer in her wonderful old hymn, "Ho! Every One That Is Thirsty."

Child of the kingdom be filled with the Spirit!
Nothing but fullness thy longing can meet;
'Tis the enduement for life and for service;
Thine is the promise, so certain, so sweet.

I will pour water on him that is thirsty,
I will pour floods upon the dry ground;
Open your hearts for the gifts I am bringing;
While ye are seeking Me, I will be found.

Who Are You?

Reputation is who people think you are. Character is who you really are.

Opinions other people have about us are unimportant. However, if you live a quality life, most people will think well of you. The key is that we are not to live with the concern of what others think of us. Our primary goal is to live so that God thinks well of us. Our goal should be to hear the words of our Lord on the day of eternal rewards: "Well done thou good and faithful servant."

God knows us intimately. He knows the complete truth about us. He knows our character. He knows who we really are.

There are declarations in the Scriptures clearly stating who we are in Christ by faith. We have to act on those proclamations of our Christian character for them to be true in our lives. For example, the Bible tells us that Christ paid the price for our sin so that "in him we might become the righteousness of God." (2 Corinthians 5:21)

Here is a statement of our Christian character: It is that we really are "the righteousness of God in Christ."

Living in that revelation of how God sees us if we have given ourselves to Him at the cross of Jesus, may sometimes be injurious to our reputation. Remember, reputation is what the world thinks of us. Character is who we truly are and that identifies the true believer with Christ.

He knows us. He knows us well. He knows our name. He knows the very number of hairs on our head (indicating how intimately He knows us).

How He values us is far more important than any opinion the world around us may have.

The highest level of character to which we can aspire is to be like Him. That is His ultimate desire for our character.

Fear Not

Jesus said many times, "Do not fear." It was His response to concerns about the past, the present, and the future.

Faith is the antidote to fear. Someone said, "When Fear knocks at your door, let Faith answer." Our confidence in our Lord is our faith and if you will put your trust in Him and His word, fear will not defeat you!

To the young girl who was to give birth to the Savior, the angel said, "Fear not."

To the shepherds in the field as they were awestruck by the appearance of a host of angels, the message was, "Fear not."

The coming of Jesus into the world and into your life is a declaration that you do not have to live in bondage to fear! Jesus came to destroy the works of the devil (1 John 3:8) and that includes destroying fear.

When you leave the doctor's office after a crushing diagnosis of illness, His word to you is "Do not fear ..." When your closest and most treasured relationships start crumbling, His message to you is "Do not fear ..." When you are being unfairly and harshly judged and events are spiraling out of your control, His message to you is "Do not fear ..."

Fourteen times in the four Gospels, the Lord used this statement, "Fear not." That is how important it is for you to recognize it is His message to you today.

Whatever issues and problems you are dealing with today put your trust and faith in your Savior and you will be able to face them without fear!

Jesus' message is a message of hope, love, trust, and faith! He wants you to have victory in your life over doubt, unbelief, and fear.

One of the greatest things Jesus said is a personal message to each one of us. In Luke 12:32, it is recorded that Jesus said, "Fear not, little flock, it is your Father's good pleasure to give you the kingdom." (ESV)

Two Ways

Scripture makes it clear there are two ways of life. One is the right way—the other is the wrong way. We can choose which of the two we take.

Jesus said, "You can enter God's Kingdom only through the narrow gate. The highway to hell is broad, and its gate is wide for the many who choose that way. But the gateway to life is very narrow and the road is difficult and only a few ever find it." (Matthew 7:13-14 NLT)

Jesus defines the two ways as a narrow way and a broad way.

John the Apostle writes that there is a way of light and a way of darkness. (Read chapter one of 1 John.) In fact, John makes it very clear that you can only walk in one path. The choice must be made between the right way that John calls the way of Light and the wrong way which he calls the way of darkness.

In addition to knowing there are two ways, it is important for us to know that we can choose the path that we will take. You have the ability to make a choice. And everyone does make that choice.

The narrow way—the way of light—leads us to eternal life on a victorious path. The broad way—the way of darkness—leads to defeat and destruction.

If you have not yet come to the time of making that choice, you will. As you stand at the crossroads of decision and you see the two paths that stretch ahead of you, you will realize you must choose one path. There are two paths before you but you can only walk down one of them.

Make sure you choose the right way. The right path will lead you to the destination everyone desires to reach. The wrong will take you to a place where no one wants to go.

There are two ways. There are two destinations. Make sure you choose the right path. When you do, you will be choosing the right destination.

Mercy

How many times have you heard someone say, "Give me what I deserve." It makes me think of the adage, "Be careful what you ask for because you may get it."

The last thing most of us should ask for is to get what we deserve.

The Bible says that sin deserves death. Additionally, it says we are sinners. (Romans 6:23 and 3:23)

Mercy is the gift that we have not earned and therefore do not deserve. God has shown mercy to all of us by enacting a perfect plan for our redemption from sin.

Mercy is not what we should expect. Sin is blight on the soul and on all humanity. However, God has shown us mercy even in our sins.

According to the Word of God, we all were guilty and dead in trespasses and sins. "But God is so rich in mercy, and he loved us so much, that even though we were dead because of our sins, he gave us life when he raised Christ from the dead." (Ephesians 2:4-5 NLT)

God's mercy! What a great gift our Father gives us in His mercy and grace.

Mercy is "compassion or forbearance shown especially to an offender." It also means "a blessing that is an act of divine favor or compassion." These dictionary definitions only come close to expressing all that mercy is to the redeemed child of God. Our experience of God's mercy surpasses any attempt to define this great declaration of God's personal love to us.

Favor undeserved and unearned is showered on us because of the wonderful mercy of God.

Jesus spoke about the man who cried out in prayer, "Oh God, be merciful to me, for I am a sinner." (Luke 18:13 NLT) We should praise the Lord that He shows His love to us by His mercy. He has freely given us a Savior. Because He loves us, He shows us His mercy every day.

"I will sing of the mercies of the Lord forever." (Psalm 89:1 NKJV)

Praise the Lord

Everyone knows this. We should praise the Lord and thank Him faithfully. However, so many of us fail to do it.

Every day is a cause for rejoicing and praising Him. Praise Him for this day! "This is the day which the Lord hath made; we will rejoice and be glad in it." (Psalm 118:24 KJV)

Paul said to the Thessalonians, " ...in everything give thanks (praise Him); for this is the will of God in Christ Jesus for you." (1 Thessalonians 5:18 NKJV)

Jesus healed ten lepers on one occasion. After healed, they went to show themselves to the priests because that was the protocol for them to return to society. Nine of them rushed away. Only one of them turned and paused to give thanks to the Lord Jesus for his healing!

Thankfulness by one out of ten may not be typical. I hope not. However, it does illustrate the point that we can so easily receive wonders from the Lord and not take the time to praise Him for His blessings.

When multitudes praised Jesus, declaring He was the Son of God, the envious Pharisees called on Him to rebuke the people who were so loudly and joyfully praising Him. Jesus replied, "If these were silent, the very stones would cry out." (Luke 19:40 ESV)

The Lord will be praised! If we leave it to others in His creation, we lose the benefits that come to us by our participation in exalting

Him. We should join our voices and hearts with all He has created and praise His holy name.

"Praise the LORD! ... Praise him according to his excellent greatness!" (Psalm 150:1-2 ESV)

"Let everything that breathes, sing praises to the Lord. Praise the Lord!" (Psalm 150:6 NLT)

True Heroes

We use the word "hero" very loosely today. Almost any good deed can get one the designation "hero." But the real hero is "the person who is recognized for great or brave acts or fine qualities."

"Great or brave acts." We immediately think of those who put their lives in jeopardy for the sake of others. The person who braves danger to rescue another person in life threatening need is a hero. We think of the many who in a time of war sacrificed their own safety to save their comrades. The military calls it "above and beyond the call of duty."

Then there are the everyday heroes. There is the mother or father who devotes a life to caring for a handicapped child. There is the spouse who holds on with the beloved spouse who has faded into unknowing but still needs care. There is the person who gives himself to help the needy at the cost of his own well being.

One of my most admired personal heroes is the Apostle Paul. He suffered great trials for his faith but he remained faithful to the Christ who met him on the road to Damascus and transformed him from a hater of Jesus to one of His most devoted followers.

For the sake of Jesus, Paul was imprisoned, stoned, whipped, shipwrecked, and severely persecuted. Traitorous brethren maligned him. They accused him of preaching false doctrine. But in all attacks, Paul stood firm for Christ.

At the time of his departure from this life, this hero of the faith said, "I have fought a good fight, I have finished my course, I have kept the faith." (2 Timothy 4:7 KJV)

Fight the good fight. Don't give up. Stand firm.

Finish the race you have started. Finish strong! Don't quit!

Keep the faith. Be true to God and His word. Hold the torch of truth high.

You can be one of God's heroes.

The Carpenter

Although I did not write this, I wanted to share for its powerful meaning.

Once upon a time, two brothers who lived on adjoining farms fell into conflict. It was the first serious rift in 40 years of farming side-by-side.

Then the long harmony fell apart. It began with a small misunderstanding, it grew into a major difference, and finally, it exploded into an exchange of bitter words followed by weeks of silence.

One morning there was a knock on John's door. He opened it to find a man with a carpenter's toolbox. "I'm looking for a few days work," he said. "Perhaps you would have a few small jobs here and there I could help with?"

"Yes," said the older brother. "I do have a job for you. Look across the creek at that farm. That's my neighbor. In fact, it's my younger brother! Last week there was a meadow between us. He recently took his bulldozer to the river levee and now there is a creek between us. Well, he may have done this to spite me, but I'll do him one better. See that pile of lumber by the barn? I want you to build me an 8-foot fence so I won't need to see his place or his face anymore."

229

The carpenter said, "I think I understand the situation. Show me the nails and the post-hole digger and I'll be able to do a job that pleases you."

The older brother had to go to town so he helped the carpenter get the materials ready and then he left for the day. The carpenter worked hard all that day. About sunset when the farmer returned, the carpenter had just finished his job.

The farmer's eyes opened wide, his jaw dropped. There was no fence there at all.

It was a bridge. A bridge that stretched from one side of the creek to the other! A fine piece of work—handrails and all! His younger brother was coming toward them with his hand outstretched.

"You are quite a fellow to build this bridge after all I've said and done."

The two brothers stood at each end of the bridge and then they met in the middle taking each other's hand. They turned to see the carpenter hoist his toolbox onto his shoulder.

"No, wait! Stay a few days. I've a lot of other projects for you," said the older brother.

"I'd like to stay on," the carpenter said, "but I have many more bridges to build."

(Author Unknown)

Thinking Back

I recently had another birthday. It was just one more in a series of many. These days I get nostalgic at the time of my birthday. It is hard for me not to reflect on the past when I have that glaring reminder that another year has passed.

Sometimes I canvas the years in my thoughts and I wonder what I would do differently in my life if I had that opportunity.

Some things I am sure I would change if I could relive the past. I would need to start with the benefit of the understanding that I have about life and myself today.

I know I would love more. I would show greater love to my family. I would love others with a deeper commitment to be helpful to any in need.

I would stay committed to any cause that I ever found worthy of my dedication. Once I knew that my cause was just, I would never waver in supporting it. And I would act with fiercer determination to maintain my resolve to never give up once I started a righteous cause.

I would always tell the truth and always defend the truth. Always.

Every person needs to find a great cause which to commit himself. I found that cause in the Gospel of Christ. However, if I were reliving my past, I would increase and intensify my dedication to the cause of Christ. Even today, as late as I may be with it, I'm trying to deepen my resolve to His truth.

I would avoid jealousy and envy. Life has taught me that these emotions severely damage the one who harbors them. They do not harm the person toward whom they are directed but they devastate the person who bears them within himself. I would always forgive quickly and completely.

Now I know I cannot relive even one hour of the past. Therefore, my decision is to view my life as the Apostle Paul viewed his. "Forgetting what lies behind and straining forward to what lies ahead, I press on toward the goal for the prize of the upward call of God in Christ Jesus." (Philippians 3:13-14 ESV)

Salvation Prayers

One of the most powerful things anyone can say to me is "I am praying for you." I know some people just use that expression as a toss away comment. But when someone tells me that and I know it is true, it is a strong encouragement to my faith.

My experience tells me the power of someone praying for me. When I was just a young boy and did not know the Lord, I went to a Vacation Bible School because I had nothing else to do in the summer. Several of the young people who attended the VBS realized that I needed to be saved. They banded together agreeing to pray for me. I did not know this until quite some time later after I had come to the Lord. One day one of those praying young people called me to tell me this.

I believe that the prayers of those young people, who took me on their heart to pray for my salvation, influenced my decision to receive the Lord in my life. This is something I have remembered through all the years and it is something I will never forget.

People who hardly knew me cared enough for me to pray for my salvation. Because of this I have been a Christian most of my life.

I have taken this experience as a guide. Now I pray regularly for those persons that I know who need to come to the Lord. Family, friends—even those whom I do not know personally, are included in my prayers for their salvation.

I encourage you to pray for others. Especially pray for those not yet saved. God wants to save those who haven't yet received Him. Therefore, when you pray for any person to be saved, you know you are praying the will of God. (2 Peter 3:9)

Justified

It is amazing that anyone could be seen as guiltless for his past no matter what he has done. However, that is exactly what the term "Justified" means in the Scriptures.

The great Scripture verse that declares this truth is in Romans 5:1. It says, "Therefore, since we are justified (acquitted, declared righteous and given a right standing with God) through faith, let us grasp the fact that we have peace with God through our Lord Jesus Christ." (AMP)

"Justified," means that God forgives our sins and sees us as righteous. That is remarkable. God considers us as one who has not sinned when He justifies us by faith through the blood of Jesus.

How can God do that? He can do it because He put the consequences of sin on Jesus on the Cross. That is what the Bible means when it says "God made Christ, who never sinned, to be the offering for our sin, so that we could be made right with God through Christ." (2 Corinthians 5:21 NLT)

This is profound truth. At the same time, it is simple. We sang about it in Sunday School as children. "Jesus loves me this I know; For the Bible tells me so." (By Anna Bartlett Warner)

The fact is that God our Father sees us as being without sin because He looks at us through Jesus. That means He has justified you. That can only be done because Jesus has paid the horrible penalty for sin. Because of that, Our Father forgives our sins and can see us as being without sin.

Justification gives us peace with God. The first verse I gave you (Romans 5:1) tells us we have peace with God because we have been justified by our faith in Him.

Justified and given peace with God. That is what we can have by faith!

Encouraging Words

Two men were talking. One of them said, "I'm going to move out west." "Why?" asked the second man. "Because," he said, "I heard the song that says, 'Home, home on the range, where the deer and the antelope play. Where seldom is heard a discouraging word, and the skies are not cloudy all day.'"

The man was looking for an ideal place. There is no such place where discouragement cannot occur. However, we can make our own location—the place where we are now—a place where no discouraging word is heard. That is in our own control!

We ought never to speak words of discouragement. None of us would if we gave enough prior thought to the words we speak. We should always be sure that anything we say is encouraging. Find that encouragement in God's word and speak it!

The words you speak have a lot to do with creating the environment around you.

Speak positive words and you will encourage yourself. Make sure your words are uplifting and filled with faith. Doing this will keep you encouraged and strengthened.

Such positive statements will also encourage others around you as they hear the declarations of encouragement from you. Encouraging words will lift you up; they will lift others around you as well.

Grumbling, complaining, criticizing—words in these categories will never lift you or others. Make sure the things you say are never negative. Speak words that are words of faith. They are words that will encourage and not discourage.

Jesus said, "What you say flows from what is in your heart." (Luke 6:45 NLT) Make sure the word of the Lord fills your heart. You will speak what is in your heart.

> "May the words of my mouth
> And the meditation of my heart
> Be pleasing to you, O LORD,
> My rock and my redeemer." (Psalm 19:14 NLT)

The Good Neighbor

Recently I preached a message to our church that I called "The Good Neighbor," based on the parable in Luke 1:25-37. This parable is commonly called, "The Good Samaritan." However, it is about three categories of people.

Bandits attacked a man on a journey. They assaulted, robbed, and left the man for dead. Two very religious men ignored him as they passed. One of them went out of his way to avoid him. Then another person came along and saw the wounded man. He stopped to help. He went the extra mile by pledging to pay the costs of the man's recovery.

The robbers who attacked the traveler and took all his possessions were the people who say, "What is yours is mine—I will take it." Many people are like this. They will take anything you have just because they have the strength to do it.

However, there are other predators who are just as bad. They may act within the law but their actions are morally abominable. Those who pillage benefits without regard for the rights and needs of others are spiritually bankrupt.

A second class, represented by the priest and the Levite (the leading religious people of their day) say, "What is mine is mine. I will keep it." These people live their insulated lives ignoring opportunities to help their neighbors who are in need. The message from Jesus is that religion does not meet people's needs.

Thankfully, there is a third viewpoint. The Samaritan man who helped the victim and met his needs represents it. This man said, "What is mine is yours. I will give it." This person is a servant. Jesus taught us that service is the path to greatness.

Fellowship.2

(On June 26 a very good friend of mine went to heaven. Dean Frost was a believer who was close to me and loved me as I loved him in Christ. This column was the one he always told me was his favorite of all the columns I have written for Clay Today. In his memory I publish this column again today.)

On a cold winter evening, two Christian men were warming themselves sitting before a cozy fireplace. They were discussing their Christian life and experiences.

The younger man expressed the reasons he did not believe attending church services was important to his Christian experience. The older, more experienced man listened carefully to the younger man's excuses. By this time the flames of the fire had diminished and only the glowing coals were left in the fireplace.

Carefully the older man reached out with the fireplace poker and pulled one coal away from the rest of the glowing coals. The one coal, separated from the others, was alone on the hearth. The fire in the single coal quickly died and instead of a bright red glow, the coal became cold and grey.

Nothing needed to be said. The younger man got the message.

When we separate ourselves from the fellowship of Christian believers, we give up one of the great benefits of the Christian life. The fellowship of other believers is one of the invisible strengths that

God has given His people. In corporate worship, we draw strength from the Lord by the encouragement of one to another.

One of the most powerful statements the Apostle John made is recorded in his first epistle. He says if we walk in the light of Jesus' presence and teaching "we have fellowship with each other, and the blood of Jesus, His Son, cleanses us from all sin." (1 John 1:7 NLT)

The fellowship of Christian believers is a gift of the Father to His children. We deprive ourselves of God's best when we do not meet faithfully with others who share our love for the Lord.

This is why we are taught in the Scriptures to continue assembling ourselves together and exhorting one another with encouragement. (Hebrews 10:25) It is signally important that you meet with fellow Christians to worship together and encourage each other.

October – November – December

Cast Your Cares Away

A promise recorded in the Bible is a great encouragement to us. "There remains a rest for the people of God." (Hebrews 4:9 NKJV) After the labor and toils of our lives are completed, God has a plan for us to rest.

This, of course, is an encouragement. It tells us the Lord has planned for our eternal well-being and prepared a wonderful place as our eternal home.

But more than that, the words of this promise tell us that we can rest in Him now! We don't have to wait for our translation to Heaven.

When you have "cast all your care upon Him," (1 Peter 5:7) as He invites you to do, you are experiencing His rest for today! When I wrote this Scripture, I misspelled it. Inadvertently I wrote, "Cast all *you are* upon Him." I left out the "r" in your and the "c" in care. Do you see it? "Cast all you *R*" (are) upon Him. So, cast all *your care* upon Him and cast all *you are* upon Him. That is true rest.

When you accept His invitation to "Come unto me all ye that labor and are heavy laden," you are assured of His promise that goes with the invitation " ...and I will give you rest" (Matthew 11:28 KJV)

Today let Him have your cares, confusions, uncertainties, and all the issues and problems of your life. There is a Savior who is willing to bear the load of life with you! You do not have to walk alone! You do not have to suffer without help!

In years past when oxen were used for plowing and towing, owners sometimes could not afford a matched pair. They had to team a mature, stronger ox with a younger, perhaps weaker one. To balance the burden, they used an adjustable yoke. The adjustment gave the shorter part of the yoke to the larger ox and the longer part of the yoke to the smaller ox. It gave the stronger ox less leverage and the younger ox more leverage to pull their loads. It put the greater part of the work load on the stronger ox and thereby actually balanced the work of the two.

Your Lord is yoked together with you. What you cannot carry, He can. When you feel you are overburdened and just cannot go on, remember your Savior is teamed with you and He is in the yoke to bear the greatest part of the load.

He will not allow more to come upon you than you are able to bear ... with His wonderful and loving help. Remember, you are not alone! He is with you to give you rest ... today, tomorrow, and forever!

Difficult Roads We Travel

The road you travel in service to Christ may be difficult and arduous. Jesus warned us it would be so.

Andrew Murray was born in South Africa. After finishing his education in England, he went to the home of his heart and he ministered the Gospel in Africa for sixty-eight years. It was not an easy road for him. Africa was a hard land in those days. Murray was a great writer on the "deeper life" of living for Christ. He was instrumental in the South African revival of 1860. Still today, his writings influence many.

When Hitler's monstrous Third Reich reigned in Germany, Dietrich Bonheoffer, a faithful German pastor, was persecuted. His life's motto guided him: "When Christ calls a man, He calls him to come and die." He faithfully preached God's Word in spite of constant opposition. Even after being confined to a Nazi concentration camp, where they later executed him, he did not stop preaching God's Word. It was not an easy road for him but he persevered to victory.

Read 2 Corinthians 11:24-26. The Apostle Paul lists much of the suffering he endured while he walked the road of service to Jesus. Paul did not believe the Lord had turned against him because that path was difficult. In fact, he rejoiced in the opportunity. Hardships and persecution never deterred Paul.

If you are on a difficult journey right now, be encouraged. Your rough road will not always be so. God's delay is not His denial. In

His plan for you, the hard road you are on now may bring you to a great, victorious destination.

The grace that brings you through your difficult times can prepare you for any trial that you may face. In the hardest of times, you will be victorious.

Heaven

It seems near death experiences have significantly increased. This is the claim that is made that a person has died or nearly died and returned to life after seeing Heaven.

It is not my purpose to validate or deny such experiences. I just have a few comments to make on this phenomenon.

We do know that spurious claims have been made about such "trips to Heaven." One recent claim was in fact revealed as a hoax apparently perpetrated to make money on a book. That does not necessarily mean that none of them are real.

It seems that the Apostles and early Christians did not need such experiences to confirm their faith. The Apostle Paul did once refer to a man who was caught up into the third Heaven but this man saw and "he heard things that cannot be told, which man may not utter." In other words, he experienced things that cannot be expressed in our earthly languages. (2 Corinthians 12 ESV)

I will say directly to you that you do not need someone's report of a trip to Heaven to confirm that Heaven is a real place. You have the best assurance you could ever have in the words of the Savior.

Jesus said, "There is more than enough room in my Father's home. If this were not so, would I have told you that I am going to prepare a place for you?" He went on to promise, "If I go and prepare a place for you, I will come back and take you to be with me that you also may be where I am." (John 14:2-3 NLT, NIV)

You do not need someone to go and come back from Heaven to confirm that it is real. Jesus' words with His promise are enough for that assurance.

God's word is more certain than anything that can be reported from one's personal experience today. You don't have to go to Heaven to know it is real!

At His ascension forty days after the resurrection, He gave proof of a new, eternal home. Jesus is all the proof you need!

That Name!

In the Bible, the Name of Jesus is declared the Name above all names. In fact, Paul states the assurance as he wrote to the Philippians that the time would come when the glory of that exalted Name will be universal. Paul said because Jesus obediently died on the cross for the sins of all mankind ...

> "God elevated him to the place of highest honor
> and gave him the name above all other names,
> that at the name of Jesus every knee should bow,
> in heaven and on earth and under the earth,
> and every tongue confess that Jesus Christ is Lord,
> to the glory of God the Father." (Philippians 2:9-11 NLT)

You cannot be true to the teaching of the Scripture without believing that there is only one Name that God the Father has exalted above all other names in history.

Jesus Christ is that Name!

Every knee in Heaven, Earth, and the underworld will bow to the Name of Jesus.

Every tongue in Heaven, Earth, and the underworld will confess that Jesus Christ is the Name of the Lord.

This Name has been given for forgiveness of sins, for divine healing, for accessing the throne of the Father, and for power to live a victorious life.

Jesus Christ lives His resurrection life in us if we are redeemed by Him. Personal salvation means that we have a relationship with Him because of the access His name gives us to the throne of God.

Every person who has put his faith in Christ has been given boldness to enter the very presence of the Living God. We have this access in His Name. "And so, dear brothers and sisters, we can boldly enter heaven's Most Holy Place because of the blood of Jesus." (Hebrews 10:19 NLT)

Great in Weakness

One of the greatest hymns ever written is, "There is a Fountain." The words are powerful! The first verse says:

There is a fountain filled with blood
Drawn from Immanuel's veins
And sinners plunged beneath that flood
Lose all their guilty stains.

William Cowper wrote and published the hymn in 1772. Millions have sung it in these ensuing years and still in worship today.

Many things about Cowper's life were sad. His mother died in childbirth when William was five years old. Older boys tormented him in his early school years. His frailties became even more apparent as the years passed.

Emotionally tormented, he was committed to mental institutions twice in his life. He made several suicide attempts. However, through all these trials he continued to write the blessed poetry of his Savior.

The wonderful thing is that his poems and hymns still live today to bless multitudes of people.

He was a friend and colleague of John Newton, the former slave ship captain, who wrote the beautiful hymn, "Amazing Grace." Newton and Cowper collaborated on many hymns and jointly published them. Even so, Cowper's emotional struggles and fears continued to plague him.

No matter how strong the emotional, spiritual, mental attacks against him were, he continued to contribute great poetry to the annals of faith by his talented—even inspired—writing.

God used the life of this man, in spite of his mental depression and spiritual doubts, to pen words that have been an inspiration to the church for 200 years. The Holy Spirit has used these words to encourage many saints and to call sinners to find their peace with God. This is peace that can only be found in that "fountain filled with blood, drawn from Immanuel's veins."

> Dear dying Lamb, Thy precious blood
> Shall never lose its pow'r,
> Till all the ransomed church of God
> Are safe, to sin no more.

Our Word

God says that He honors His word above His name. He actually says in Psalm 138:2 that His promises are backed by all the honor of His name. That is a lofty standard and it shows the value that the Lord puts on the integrity of His word.

I do not propose that we can reach a standard that high. However, I do say that your integrity should back your words and keeping your promises is a measure of your integrity!

We live by our words and the promises we make to others. A marriage contains vows. Vows are promises. To have a successful marriage you must live by those promises.

Colleges have honor codes. Those codes are promises made. Negative results follow the discovery of students breaking that code.

There was a time when men valued their word and were disgraced in society when they broke it. They were said to be, "a man of his word." It meant when that person made a statement or a promise to anyone, it was considered as dependable as a legal contract.

What about promises you have made to God? They usually start this way: "Lord, if you will just do this thing for me, I will (you know what you promised)." Make this right with God if you have said things you failed to do.

I still expect people to keep their word. I do not expect anyone to lie to me. I know this is an idealistic expectation. However, I know the Apostle Paul taught us not to lie, which means being true to our word.

If you want your testimony to be a strong witness for Christ, live by your word. Be true to yourself and God and everyone who interacts with you will know you are a person of integrity.

Loving Jesus

One morning, Simon Peter and six of the other Apostles decided to go fishing. Jesus had risen from the dead and He had appeared to them twice, having appeared to Peter in a one-on-one encounter. Now He appeared to these men for the third time.

In the very early morning, they saw Jesus standing on the beach. When they recognized Him, Peter jumped in the water and swam to Him. The others brought the boat in to shore and they all gathered around the fire that Jesus had started. Then they saw that Jesus, always a servant, had cooked breakfast for them.

After they had eaten, Jesus spoke to Peter. "Do you love me, Simon?" Simon Peter answered, "Yes, Lord, I love you."

Again, Jesus asked Peter, "Simon, do you love me?" Once more, he answered, "Yes, Lord, I love you."

Jesus asked him a third time, "Do you love me, Simon?" Peter answered a third time and said, "Lord, you know that I love you."

Each time Peter answered, "Yes" and each time Jesus said, "Feed my sheep." Jesus was directing Peter to demonstrate his love by serving His people.

Jesus taught a very clear way of demonstrating our love for Him. He said, "Those who accept my commandments and obey them are the ones who love me." (John 14:21 NLT)

Regardless of how many times we say we love Him, the only way we can truly declare it is by keeping His Word. If we love Him, we are serving Him. It is not enough simply to say we love the Lord. The real evidence of our love is our keeping His word.

John wrote, "And this is love: that we walk in obedience to his commands." (2 John 1:6 NIV)

He has asked you the same question He asked Peter. What was your answer?

Hold On

Henry Dempsey was a pilot flying a commuter flight from Portland, Maine to Boston. When he heard an unusual noise in the back of the aircraft, he asked his co-pilot to take over as he went to check out the source of the noise.

A rear door not properly latched before takeoff caused the mysterious noise. When the aircraft hit some turbulence, Mr. Dempsey leaned against the door, hinged at the bottom, and the stairway door opened. He tumbled forward, grabbed the railings as he fell, and lay upside down on the stairs as the plane cruised at 190 miles per hour at an altitude of 4,000 feet.

Seeing the red light that indicated an open door, the co-pilot radioed the nearest airport requesting an emergency landing. He thought the pilot had fallen out of the plane. However, when the plane landed, they found Henry Dempsey holding on to the railings of the stairway door.

The co-pilot did not realize Dempsey was hanging on until the plane was on the ground.

This is a true story. New York Times published it on September 3, 1987.

When it seems like the bottom has dropped out from beneath you, you have only two choices—hold on or let go.

Don't let go! Hold on to God's promises in His Word like never before.

When your heart is breaking over a great loss and you cannot understand "Why" – hold on!

When you have been misused, falsely accused, and betrayed – hold on!

When your life seems to be falling apart, you are discouraged, and want to hide from the world – hold on!

There is no other good choice. If you let go, you lose. If you hold on, you win.

You cannot win if you quit. If you hold on, God will give you a safe landing!

Decisions

After a great effort to find a job, a man was hired to work in a packing plant. Assigned a place on a conveyor line, he was to look carefully at the potatoes that passed before him. According to the size of each potato, decide if it was to be put in the basket of select premium quality potatoes or if it was to go into a basket of lesser size and quality.

When a few days had passed, he went to his foreman and announced he was quitting. "Why are you quitting? Surely the work is not too hard or strenuous," the foreman said. "Oh no. It is not hard work at all," the man replied. "It is all those decisions that are killing me."

We must make decisions every day. The quality of the choices we make today may determine the course of our future. Success or failure tomorrow may come from decisions we make today.

I have seen many people walk forward to an altar to receive Christ as Savior. Then they quickly fade away from the fellowship of God's people. After making the decision, I believe that some people reconsider and do not want to pay the price of following Jesus Christ after all.

Jesus explained it in the parable of The Sower in Matthew 13:18-23. Sometimes people "make decisions" when they have not really decided! Your conclusion to follow Christ and live for him must be firm and irrevocable.

In Jesus' ministry on earth, there were many who were called to follow Him. Many accepted that call; many did not. It is still true today. For many the decision to "leave all" and follow Him is a price too steep. For many others there is no price too great to follow Him.

The best choice you can make, even though it may be a difficult one, is to become His disciple and follow Him.

Always Right?

Some folks are never wrong. Whatever opinion they have is always the right one. When there are various opinions on an issue, theirs is always correct.

We certainly should be firm in our righteous convictions. However, we should not be hardened in self-righteousness.

Jesus taught us humility. We need to understand that. I believe the Apostle Paul did understand it. In the King James Version of the Bible, he said, "I say to everyone among you not to think of himself more highly than he ought to think." (Romans 12:3) Another Scripture version puts it this way: None of us should "have an exaggerated opinion of his own importance." (Romans 12:3 AMP)

Today the repetitive "gospel of ME" misleads many people into believing they are not just one of God's chosen ones but that they are God's chosen ONE.

Wrong thinking about God will cause you to devalue yourself. Wrong thinking about yourself will cause you to devalue God.

Some people think they are better at their job than any fellow workers are. Some think they are better singers than anyone else in the choir is. Some think they are the best usher on the team.

You do not understand why someone around you is always causing a problem. Yet you are always there in the middle of the problem. Doesn't that tell you anything?

Someone told me a bad spirit followed him to every church where he went. If a wrong spirit is always where you are, what does that tell you? As a famed columnist said, "Wake up and smell the coffee!"

In many sports, they have a Most Valuable Player award. Do you know that a new person is selected for that award every season?

I am not suggesting that we devalue ourselves. I am saying that we ought not to devalue others as we elevate ourselves. Be the person God has called you to be and serve in the place that God has put you. When you do that in the spirit of humility that Jesus taught, the Lord Himself will elevate you, and that is the best status that anyone can ever receive.

The Power of Two

Sometimes Jesus said things that shock me when I read them. One of these challenging statements of Jesus is this: "I say to you, if two of you agree on earth about anything they ask, it will be done for them by my Father in heaven." (Matthew 18:19 ESV)

Several years ago, a brother in Christ came to me about prayer. He asked me if I would join him in praying that his brother-in-law would accept Christ as his Savior. We talked about it for a while. We both agreed that this man really needed salvation. And we committed to praying for Him to accept the Lord.

We began to pray at the same time daily - 6 AM - for his salvation. In those days, 6 AM was a challenge to me. Nevertheless, I dutifully arose every morning and joined my friend in praying for his brother-in-law. We prayed for weeks. Frequently we would speak about our prayer times and encourage each other as we continued to pray and believe. Encouraging each other kept us praying and committed to believe for the man's salvation. That is the power of two.

One Sunday night we were in the regular church service. My prayer partner was there. I was there as the pastor of the church. Unlike his normal habits, the brother-in-law was there, too. I don't think I had ever seen him in a Sunday evening service before. When I finished preaching and extended an invitation for those who wanted to receive the Lord to come forward, he stepped out into the aisle and walked to the altar. That night he received the Lord.

He walked with the Savior until he died a few years ago. My friend who joined me in prayer for him saw him the night before he went to Heaven. A few days ago, my friend reminded me of this. He said that night he held his brother-in-law's hand as he said, "I am ready to meet my Lord."

Two men joined in prayer for a hardened man who was far from God, to come to the Savior. God answered their prayer of agreement.

Jesus said, "If any two of you agree" in prayer I will answer. It is the power of two. There is someone who will agree with you in faith and prayer for the answer you need!

God's Word: Believe It; Live It

Many folks read with a question mark, some of the things that are very clear in the Bible. They don't want to believe the simple message so they throw up barriers. Maybe they just will not read it because they know it does not say what they want it to say.

If you want to live a victorious life, it is dangerous to fail to read and know God's Word. If you do not read the Bible, you obviously do not want the Lord to lead you or to speak to you.

If I mailed you a letter with instructions that you need and said you wanted, what would you do with it? Would you put it aside to read sometime later (maybe) or would you read it immediately knowing it contains the valuable information you need?

We believe the Bible is God's Word. If it is God's Word, it is a tremendous loss to ignore it.

If you do not believe it, I need to write another column for you. Today this message is for those who say they believe the Bible is God's Word.

I believe it. Moreover, I believe that every answer we need in life is contained in His Word. It has been given to us to guide us in our lives as the Holy Spirit teaches it to us.

We want to know the will of God. His Word tells us. (Read 1 John 2:15-17.) The last part of this passage says, "Whoever does the will of God abides forever." The preceding verses tell us about knowing and doing God's will.

How do we get closer to the Lord? Again, the Word tells us. "Come close to God and He will come close to you." (James 4:8 NLT)

If you make any important decision without clearly consulting God's Word and waiting on the Holy Spirit, you are failing to use the resources God has given you to be able to know His will.

Sometimes we fail to read His Word because we don't really want to know what He is saying. If we know, we are responsible to do it. However, failing to know His will does not relieve you of any responsibility.

He has made it clear to us that His Word will reveal His will!

Persevere

Call it determination, or perseverance, or a "stick to it" attitude. There are people who make a commitment and refuse to quit until their promise is fulfilled. The Bible is full of narratives of those who quit and those who refused to quit.

Demas left Paul. John Mark left Barnabas and Paul while on their first missionary journey. Judas deserted Jesus. They were quitters. There are people who are willing to give up while others determine to "stay the course."

In his epistles, Paul speaks of numerous men who stayed with him through suffering and imprisonment until the very end.

Why do some people quit before the race is completed? They become discouraged. They become disappointed. They become disillusioned.

Some are quitting every day. They quit on their education. They quit on their marriage and family. They quit on their friends and their church. They quit on relationships with friends and jobs. For many people it is much easier to quit than continue. It is largely because their life is all about "ME!"

Then there are those who are dependable. They can be trusted to keep their commitments.

This is about being faithful. It is about finishing the race. It is about refusing to quit. That is exactly what the Apostle Paul is speaking of when he says, "I have fought the good fight, I have finished the race, I have kept the faith." (2 Timothy 4:7 ESV)

If you quit, you give up. You surrender. However, God gives you power to persevere against any odds and live the life of victory. You can be an overcomer. "In all things we are more than conquerors through him who loved us." (Romans 8:37 ESV)

Never quit on God. He will never quit on you.

What is the person that the Lord honors – the victor or the quitter? Which one are you?

Agreement

The Old Testament Prophet, Amos, asks an intriguing question: "Can two people walk together without agreeing on the direction?" (Amos 3:3 NLT) You would not be required to agree on everything with another person in order to travel with him. However, you certainly would have to agree on the direction.

The Bible speaks a lot about unity. "How good and pleasant it is when God's people live together in unity!" (Psalm 133:1 NIV) Unity in your family, unity in the workplace, unity in the church—this can be accomplished.

We are not speaking of absolute or total agreement on all things. This spiritual unity is the agreement that causes us to coalesce around a common goal with the common purpose to achieve that goal.

Paul's statement to the Ephesian church expresses this unity so graciously. He said, "Make every effort to keep yourselves united in the Spirit, binding yourselves together with peace." (Ephesians 4:3 NLT)

To achieve this unity of agreement and cooperation, Paul wrote that we must "not insist on (our) own way." (1 Corinthians 13:5 ESV) I often paraphrase that verse as saying "we must give up the right to be right." When this spirit prevails among us, we have the unity for which the heart of God calls.

Jesus taught that unity could produce powerful prayer. He said, "I also tell you this: If two of you agree here on earth concerning anything you ask, my Father in heaven will do it for you." (Matthew 18:19 NLT)

There is superior strength when we unite our faith to touch God in prayer. God loves the spiritual unity that binds us together so much that He adds it to the power of faith for answered prayer.

Join with your wife, husband, or a friend. Find a brother or sister in Christ. Unite to support each other. Make an agreement for a spiritual goal. Lay aside anything divisive and focus your faith in unity. You will see the miracle that God does when you achieve the "unity of the Spirit in the bond of peace." (Ephesians 4:3 ESV)

The Carnal Spirit

There is a deceitful spirit at work in the world today. It is a spirit that declares to you that your self will is God's will for you.

Many people talk regularly about "being led." They are saying that they are led by the Holy Spirit. But they have been deceived into believing that what they want is what the Holy Spirit is telling them to do.

The Scriptural teaching is that we are first led into a surrendered life by the Holy Spirit. He (the Holy Spirit) teaches us that affection for self is antagonistic to being led by the Holy Spirit.

This is the Scripture Christians find it hard to embrace: "If we live by the [Holy] Spirit, let us also walk by the Spirit." (Galatians 5:25 NASB) In other words, "If by the Holy Spirit we have our life in God, let us go forward walking in line, our conduct controlled by the Spirit."

The confusion is between the "life of the flesh" and "the life of the Spirit." To Paul, "the flesh" is the nature of man that is lustful, deceitful and self absorbed. Life in the Spirit (walking in the Spirit) is living the fruit of the Spirit described in Galatians 5:22 & 23: "The fruit of the Spirit is love, joy, peace, patience, kindness, goodness, faithfulness, gentleness, self-control."

Use this guideline. When you are making a relational decision—a decision that affects your life and the lives of others—are you walking in the fruit of the Spirit?

Is there contention, argumentation, selfishness, or disharmony? If these expressions are produced in your process can you really say you are led by the Holy Spirit?

It has always amazed me when I have seen churches split and the "split" builds another church a mile from the first one. Every time I see this, I think of spiritual failure.

Carnal fruits are the opposite of being led by the Holy Spirit in our daily walk.

Our Great God

Almighty power is complete and absolute power. God is the only almighty power in the Universe. *He is omnipotent.* He has all power over all things in the Creation.

He is omniscient. He knows everything. He has unlimited understanding and knowledge.

He is omnipresent. He is in all places at all times. The psalmist said, "Where can I go from your Spirit? Where can I flee from your presence? If I go up to the heavens, you are there; if I make my bed in the depths, you are there. If I rise on the wings of the dawn, if I settle on the far side of the sea, even there your hand will guide me; your right hand will hold me fast." (Psalm 139:7-10 NIV)

He is our great God who is above all His creation. There is no way for us to fully express His power, majesty, supremacy and glory. We just have to look at Him in awe and proclaim that He is a wonderful, glorious God.

Our great God made a choice. He chose to love us. When He covered the nakedness of Adam and Eve in Eden's Garden, He declared that He will love His created man and woman even in their sin. Everything written about God in His Word is a statement of His love for us. The Cross is the ultimate statement of this fact.

Christianity is different from every other religion in this way. God Himself, not man, offers the sacrifice for man's sins. And that is a testimony of His love for His children. "But God is so rich in mercy, and he loved us so much, that even though we were dead because of our sins, he gave us life when he raised Christ from the dead." (Ephesians 2:4-5 NLT)

The great God of the universe who created galaxies of planets and stars beyond anything yet discovered by man, has chosen to love you. Today, stand in that truth.

God loves you!

Grace

This is a modern telling of the story Jesus told about the lost son. It is taken from the book "What's So Amazing About Grace?"

It is the story of a prodigal daughter who grows up in Traverse City, Michigan. Disgusted with her old fashioned parents who overreact to her nose ring, the music she listens to, and the length of her skirts, she runs away. She ends up in Detroit where she meets a man who drives the biggest car she's ever seen. The man with the big car—she calls him "Boss"—recognizes that since she's underage, men would pay a premium fee for her. So she goes to work for him. Things seem good for a while, but she gets sick for a few days and it amazes her how quickly Boss turns mean. Before she knows it, she's out on the street without a penny to her name. She still turns a couple of tricks a night and all the money goes to support her drug habit.

One night while sleeping on the metal grates of the city, she began to feel less like a woman of the world and more like a little girl.

She begins to whimper. "God, why did I leave? My dog back home eats better than I do now."

She knows that more than anything in the world, she wants to go home. Three calls home get three connections with the answering machine. Finally she leaves a message.

"Mom, dad, it's me. I was wondering about maybe coming home. I'm catching a bus up your way and it'll get there about midnight tomorrow. If you're not there, I'll understand."

During the seven hour bus ride, she prepares a speech for her father. When the bus comes to a stop in the Traverse City station, the driver announces the fifteen-minute stop. Fifteen minutes to decide her life.

She walks into the terminal not knowing what to expect. Not one of the thousand scenes that have played out in her mind prepares her for what she sees. There in the bus terminal stands a group of forty brothers and sisters, aunts and uncles and cousins, and a grandmother. They're all wearing goofy party hats and blowing noise-makers, and taped across the entire wall of the terminal is a banner that reads, "Welcome Home!"

Out of the crowd of well-wishers breaks her dad. She stares out through the tears quivering in her eyes and begins her memorized speech. He interrupts her. "Hush, child. We've got no time for that. No time for apologies. We'll be late. A big party is waiting for you at home."

Still Free

The first amendment to the Constitution of the United States guarantees the "Congress shall make no law respecting an establishment of religion, or prohibiting the free exercise thereof …" Amendment I goes on to guarantee freedom of speech, freedom of the press, the right of citizens to peacefully assemble, and the right to petition the government for grievances.

The Bill of Rights, the first ten amendments to the Constitution, were adopted because many were afraid that without them the federal government would have too much power and they wanted individual rights guaranteed in the document that would become the foundation of government in this young country.

> We hold these truths to be self-evident, that all men are created equal, that they are endowed by their Creator with certain unalienable Rights, that among these are Life, Liberty and the pursuit of Happiness.

The majestic words in the Preamble to the Declaration of Independence, state the firm conviction of our nation's founders that all of our rights of freedom and liberty are given to us by God. The conviction was that since our rights are given by God, no person or government would ever be able to cancel or even abridge them.

The dictionary definition of "unalienable" means "absolute, infrangible, inviolable, non-negotiable, nontransferable, unassignable, untransferable." The founding fathers have written voluminously that their conviction was *"inalienable" rights were rights given to us by God.*

Anything that God has given us cannot rightfully be taken from us by any person(s) or government. There is danger in our country now that rights granted us by our Sovereign God will be removed or restricted by unconstitutional actions and misguided people in authority.

This is especially true of freedom of religion. In the misnamed demand for diversity, tolerance, and acceptance, the individual's right of freedom of religion is being endangered.

America is a place like no other place in the history of the world. We must defend vigorously the rights we have been guaranteed by our Constitution. This is especially true of the right that gives us the right to worship freely.

Powerful Prayers

"The effective prayer of faith comes from a life given up to the will and the love of God. Not as a result of what I try to be when praying, but because of what I am when I'm not praying, is my prayer answered by God." ~Andrew Murray in *With Christ in the School of Prayer.*

It was the spring of 1862 and the Civil War had taken its toll. Evangelist D. L. Moody was frequently seen on the battlefields, ministering to soldiers on the frontlines. During one instance, late at night after a weary day at war, he was walking among the body-strewn fields.

Hundreds of men were wounded and famished, but a search of the area produced little nourishment for the weary men. Desperate, Moody and others prayed asking God to provide the needed supplies.

As the first gleam of morning light rose above the battlefield, a wagon appeared on the horizon. As it approached the workers, they realized it was a large farm wagon piled high with loaves of bread. God had provided: manna from heaven!

The driver approached the men and told the following story. "When I went to bed last night, I knew the army was gone and I could not sleep for thinking of the poor fellows who were wounded and would have to stay behind. Something seemed to whisper in my ear, 'What will those poor fellows do for something to eat?' I could not get rid of this voice."

That faithful servant of God could not sleep, so he woke his wife and she began baking as much bread as possible. Meanwhile, he hitched up his wagon to deliver food to the battlefield. Said the man, "I felt just as if I was being sent by our Lord Himself."

He was!

- From A Passion for Souls:
The Life of D. L. Moody by Lyle W. Dorsett

When we pray, remember:

1. The love of God that wants the best for us.
2. The wisdom of God that knows what is best for us.
3. The power of God that can accomplish it.

More Prayer

Prayer is an essential part of a Christian life. It may very well be the most important part of life for God.

Perhaps more people have spoken and written about prayer than any other subject on Christian living. Here are some things that well-known and some not-so-well-known people have said about prayer.

Fear not because your prayer is stammering, your words feeble, and your language poor. Jesus can understand you.
– J.C. Ryle

Pray often, for prayer is a shield to the soul, a sacrifice to God, and a scourge for Satan. – John Bunyan

God shapes the world by prayer. The more prayer there is in the world the better the world will be, the mightier the forces against evil. – E.M. Bounds

Don't pray when you feel like it. Have an appointment with the Lord and keep it. A man is powerful on his knees.
– Corrie Ten Boom

Talking to men for God is a great thing, but talking to God for men is greater still. – E.M. Bounds

Satan trembles when he sees the weakest Christian on his knees. – William Cowper

Prayer will make a man cease from sin or sin will entice a man to cease from prayer. – John Bunyan

Eighteen-year-old Hudson Taylor wandered into his father's library and read a gospel tract. He couldn't shake off its message. Finally, falling to his knees, he accepted Christ as his Savior. Later, his mother returned home after having been away. When Hudson told her the good news she said, "I already know. Ten days ago, the very date on which you tell me you read that tract, I spent the entire afternoon in prayer for you until the Lord assured me that my wayward son had been brought into the fold." (From Our Daily Bread, July 19, 1989) Hudson Taylor was a missionary who spent 51 years in China winning more than 125,000 people to Christ.

Overflow

Before anything can overflow, it must be full. If you want the overflowing blessings of the Lord in your life, you must first be full of Him.

This is certainly a legitimate goal and expectation. His word speaks many times of being full of Him. In fact, Paul speaks of his deep desire "that you may be filled with all **the fullness of God.**" (Ephesians 3:19 ESV)

Paul desires that "we all reach unity in the faith and in the knowledge of the Son of God and become mature, attaining to the whole measure of **the fullness of Christ.**" (Ephesians 4:13 NIV)

Once you are engaged in that wonderful standing where you are filled with His fullness, the overflow of God's blessings and favor becomes the single highlight of your daily life.

The 23rd Psalm expresses this concept so beautifully. David wrote, "My cup runneth over." That is the poetic wording of the King James Version of the Bible. Put into modern language as most of the rest of the translations do, the words are "my cup **overflows.**" That is our legitimate expectation—overflow of God's blessings and favor upon us.

Paul told us, "God will generously provide all you need. Then you will always have everything you need and plenty left over ..." (2 Corinthians 9:8 NLT)

Have you ever viewed the majestic Niagara Falls? It is a wonderful sight. It is reported that 150,000 U.S. gallons or 567,811 liters flow over the falls every second.

That flow is constant and uninterrupted. Only once was that great avalanche of water halted. The flow of water was stopped completely for several hours over both falls on March 29, 1848 due to an ice jam in the upper river. This is the only known time a stoppage occurred.

The Falls are an example of water in abundance. They are the example of God's overflow for you and there never has to be a halt in the great abundant outpouring of His blessings in your life.

Substitution

During the Civil War, in 1863, there was a draft instituted to fill the ranks of the army. The draft laws allowed for two methods for avoiding military service. The methods were substitution or commutation.

The draft lotteries chose men for mandatory military service. A man whose name was drawn could either pay a commutation fee of $300 or he could provide a substitute for himself. The substitute would exempt him from service for the duration of the war.

The draft was called the Enrollment Act. The $300 commutation fee was effective only for that particular draft. When a man found and hired a substitute—often reaching a cost of $1000 or more—he was then free from serving in the army.

To find a substitute was to find someone who was willing to give his life for you. Admittedly it was for money but it was still potentially a sacrifice of one's life for another.

In a different context, Jesus said, "Greater love has no one than this, that someone lay down his life for his friends." (John 15:13 ESV) He is speaking to His disciples and letting them know they have a special relationship with Him. He now calls them friends.

But Paul makes a declaration that is even more far reaching. He speaks of a substitute who is willing to die for those who are not even his friends. In fact, he speaks of a life given for those who are enemies when he says, "But God demonstrates his own love for us in this: While we were still sinners, Christ died for us." (Romans 5:8 NIV)

He was not paid to substitute His life for us. He died for us as a demonstration that our Heavenly Father loves us supremely. He loved us so much He gave His own Son to die in our place.

I owed a debt I could not pay.
He paid a debt He did not owe.
- "He Paid A Debt He Did Not Owe"
by Ellis J. Crum

When Jesus died on the cross for our sins, it was the greatest act of sacrificial love ever known.

True Love

The greatest chapter in the Bible on love is 1 Corinthians 13. It is here that the supremacy of love over all things is established. In the last verse, Paul writes, "Three things will last forever—faith, hope, and love—and the greatest of these is love." (NLT)

Agape love is the type of love expressed in the New Testament as "the love of God for man and of man for God." Agape is the expression of the unconditional love God has for His people. It becomes very personal when we realize the many times His Word tells us of His supreme and superior love for us.

Often very powerful and profound truth can be best expressed in simple words. The little verse from long ago comes to mind.

> He loves, He loves me, He loves me this I know;
> He gave Himself to die for me because He loves me so.
> - "He Loves Me" by Isaac Watts

The Apostle John states it so simply yet profoundly when he writes, "We love him, because he **first loved us**." (1 John 4:19 KJV)

The love we return to our Lord is best expressed in our love for others. In fact, John also states in his first letter, "He who does not love his brother whom he has seen cannot love God whom he has not seen." (1 John 4:20 ESV) So we are taught in these words that the only way we have to declare our love for God is by showing our love for others.

God loves us. We love God. We show our love for God by loving others. It seems simple. And the message is simple. Practicing it is the difficult part.

Here is practical love. Return to 1 Corinthians 13. "Love is patient and kind; love does not envy or boast; it is not arrogant or rude. It does not insist on its own way; it is not irritable or resentful; it does not rejoice at wrongdoing, but rejoices with the truth. Love bears all things, believes all things, hopes all things, endures all things." (Verses 4-7 ESV)

This is true love.

Christmas

God's Gift

This is a season for giving. It is appropriate that we express the spirit of the season by giving gifts. After all, this whole time is about the greatest gift ever given. It is about God giving His own Son as a gift for the salvation of all who will believe in Him.

Someone has given John 3:16 the title, "The World's Greatest Love Story." Love is always about giving. (John 3:16 says "For God so loved the world that he gave his only Son, that whoever believes in him should not perish but have eternal life." (ESV))

In the most powerful and poignant terms, this verse speaks of the greatest quality of a loving God. He loved us so much that He gave His own Son as the sacrifice that would take away our sins.

John the Baptist spoke of Jesus as "the lamb of God that takes away the sin of the world." (John 1:29 NKJV) Scripture says that He (Jesus) was the "Lamb (of God) slain from the foundation of the world." (Revelation 13:8 KJV)

Isaiah put it this way. "For unto us a child is born, unto us a son is given ..." (Isaiah 9:6 KJV)

Therefore, here is the message of Christmas: God loved us. His love caused Him to give His Son for our sins. Because of His great gift, we now have the gift of salvation. "For by grace you are saved through faith; and that not of yourselves: it is the gift of God." (Ephesians 2:8 WEB)

William P. Register, Sr.

When you are receiving gifts from others this season, remember that you have already received the greatest gift ever given or ever will be given.

You have the gift of salvation from God because He gave His Son for us. Thanks to God for His indescribable gift. (2 Corinthians 9:15)

This Day

"And in the same region there were shepherds out in the field, keeping watch over their flock by night. And an angel of the Lord appeared to them, and the glory of the Lord shone around them, and they were filled with great fear. And the angel said to them, 'Fear not, for behold, I bring you good news of great joy that will be for all the people. For unto you is born *This Day* (emphasis mine) in the city of David a Savior, who is Christ the Lord. And this will be a sign for you: you will find a baby wrapped in swaddling clothes and lying in a manger.'" (Luke 2:8-12 ESV)

This day ... the fullness of time had come (and) God sent forth his Son, born of woman, born under the law, to redeem those who were under the law, so that we might receive adoption as sons.

This day ... the Word was made flesh and dwelt among us.

This day ... the Son of God became the son of man so that the sons of man could become the sons of God.

This day ... Heaven gave up its Light so that the light of the world could overcome the darkness of the world.

This day ... an infant babe miraculously came out of a virgin's womb to change forever the course of the history of the world.

This day ... the King of Kings was born in a humble stable in the presence of donkeys, sheep, and other animals.

This day ... The message came forth from the halls of heaven, "This is my beloved son."

This day ... He was rich, yet for your sakes He became poor, that you through His poverty might become rich. (2 Corinthians 8:9 NKJV)

This day ... our Savior, Jesus was born!

Stand for Truth

Recently I have written about two of my offspring. The other one now has to be included. Therefore, I will tell you of a true incident that involves my first daughter, who is my middle child.

It was Christmas season and all the adults had gone shopping, except me. I had the responsibility of several young children. The parents had decided they would rather be anywhere else than with a gang of rowdy kids. My daughter, Kimberly, was about 6 or 7 years old and she was one of the ringleaders of the disturbance among the others that day.

Looking for a way to calm them, I said I was taking them to the mall to see Santa Claus. Kim rebelled. Atypical of her, she was the most uncontrollable of the gang of kids at this time. My effort to appease the gang with the Santa visit met strong resistance from her. On the way to the mall, Kim kept saying, "I don't want to see Santa; I don't even believe in him anyway; he is not real." All the while, as we left the car, she was crying and pulling on me to stop. "I don't believe in Santa; I don't want to see him," she kept crying with copious tears.

As we started walking into the mall, Kim became very silent. Looking down the long opening, she saw the red suit and white beard. I felt her pulling hard on my hand. She wanted me to stop walking. I did and as she wiped tears from her eyes, she said to me rather quietly and very seriously. "Daddy, can you tell I have been crying."

She didn't want Santa to know she had been crying. Of course, she was right in her statements of non-belief in him.

Error and untruth are prevalent in our world today. You and I must distinguish the truth from the error and take our stand for unbending truth. There are moral issues disguised as political policy.

The issues today do not include Santa Claus. I would expect such a cultural icon to impact a 6 or 7 year old, but we are adults. More than that, we should be spiritual adults proclaiming truth.

We are in a spiritual war. Let your devotional Scriptures today include Ephesians 6:10-20. Then determine that your posture will be standing for truth.

The End

Never Quit

One decision can change the course of a person's life. At every crossroads of life, we have to choose the right way or the wrong way. At those crossroads of decision, many people have chosen the wrong way and many have chosen the right way.

After he had denied Jesus in the courtyard of Pilate, Simon Peter faced the choice of turning away from Jesus or turning back to Him. To Peter's great credit he decided to stay with Jesus.

Saul of Tarsus had the chance to turn away from Jesus. Blinded for three days after his Damascus road experience, he waited for an answer from the Lord. Saul decided to stay with Jesus. He became the great apostle Paul.

During his time of service to the Lord Jesus, many men rallied to the aid of the apostle Paul and ministered to him as servants. Paul's epistles are full of the names of these men.

Among the records of these many men, there is one very sad comment. He made this statement about one of them: "Demas, in love with this present world, has deserted me and gone to Thessalonica."

Paul wrote that report in his second letter to Timothy. Demas was a man they both knew very well. When Paul wrote to the church at Colossae, he told them Demas was with him. When Paul wrote his loving letter to Philemon, he spoke of Demas as a fellow worker.

Demas was with Paul in prison. He stayed with him through hardships and suffering. Then there came a day when Demas decided he would not finish the course. He gave up. He surrendered to the enticements and pleasures of the world. That was Paul's report. It must have brought great sadness to his heart.

Demas was a quitter. When you face struggles and hardships, you have to make a decision. Demas made the wrong decision. You can make the right one.

It is always the right decision to continue following Jesus. Don't quit. Finish strong!

Our Guardian

The early American Indians had a unique practice of training young braves. On the night of a boy's thirteenth birthday, after learning about hunting, scouting, and fishing skills, he was put to one final test.

He was placed in a dense forest to spend the entire night alone. Until then, he had never been away from the security of the family and tribe. But on this night, he was blindfolded and taken several miles away. When he took off the blindfold, he was in the middle of thick woods. It had to be terrifying. Every time a twig snapped, he visualized a wild animal ready to pounce.

After what seemed like an eternity, dawn broke and the first rays of sunlight entered the interior of the forest. Looking around, the boy saw flowers, trees, and the outline of a path. Then to his utter astonishment, he beheld the figure of a man standing just a few feet away, armed with a bow and arrow. It was his father. He had been there all night long watching over his son.

I don't know if this story is true. My research has not been successful in proving it true but I love the truth it represents. Even if is not, it is an illustration of a wonderful truth that all need to know.

Whatever you may be going through, the Lord is watching over you! He is always on guard over your life if you are walking with Him.

"When you go through deep waters,
I will be with you.
When you go through rivers of difficulty,
you will not drown.
When you walk through the fire of oppression,
you will not be burned up;
the flames will not consume you." (Isaiah 43:2 NLT)

God is your Guardian and Protector!

Never Too Late

When Jesus died on the cross, He was not alone. There were worshipping women, including His mother, who had followed Him and stayed with Him through the crucifixion. His beloved Apostle John was there, too.

There were also those who were there to mock Him and rail upon Him. Among these were the thieves crucified with Him. One was on His left and the other on His right. Both of them mocked Him.

However, something happened with one of them. After first mocking Jesus, he had a change of mind and heart.

His change of mind caused him to rebuke his dying thief friend. Then he turned to Jesus and said, "Jesus, remember me when you come into your kingdom." Jesus said He would. "Today you will be with me in Paradise." (Luke 23:42-43 ESV)

It is never too late to turn to the Lord. This man only had a very short while—maybe just minutes—between accepting Jesus and the time of his death. Nevertheless, his decision for Christ is still being told today, as I am telling it to you now.

As He always does, Jesus responded to the cry of a sincere heart. This man started to live as he was dying. The greatest decision anyone ever makes is the decision to accept Jesus Christ.

Whatever your surrounding circumstances may be, the Lord will hear your sincere cry. This man could not have been in a worse situation—being executed for crimes he had committed!

Regardless of your situation today, if you sincerely call on the Lord, He will hear you. Not only will He hear you, He will answer you.

Do not let your current condition cause you to believe that the Lord is not near you. He is as close as the cry of your heart.

You need no formality or prerequisite to call on the Lord. It is as simple as saying, "Lord, remember me."

Printed in the United States
By Bookmasters